Desperadoes

The Rise and Fall of the Poe-Hart Gang

By R. D. Morgan

NEW FORUMS

Stillwater, Oklahoma
U.S.A.

This book may be ordered in bulk quantities at discount from
New Forums Press, Inc., P.O. Box 876, Stillwater, OK 74076
[Federal I.D. No. 73 1123239]. Printed in the United States of
America.

International Standard Book Number: 1-58107-063-2

Preface

The author gratefully acknowledges the assistance of the following people and organizations. Without their help, this book would never have seen the light of day. Nelda Poe Smith, Betty Poe, Teri Dotson Halsey, Joe Tucker, Archie Collins, Julie Arrowood, Jeannie Inman, and Curt Johnson; the good folks at both the Okfuskee and Nowata County Historical Museums, along with the friendly citizens of the communities of IXL, Okemah, Vinta, Nowata, and Centralia, Oklahoma. Also, a big debt of gratitude is owed to my wife, Naomi, and my publisher, Doug Dollar.

Other books by R. D. Morgan:

The Bad Boys of the Cookson Hills
New Forums Press, Inc.
Stillwater, OK
1-800-606-3766

The Bandit Kings of the Cookson Hills
New Forums Press, Inc.
Stillwater, OK
1-800-606-3766

Armed and Dangerous
EZ Lane Publishing
P. O. Box 444
Haskell, Ok 74436
Naomi777ezlane@aol.com

Table of Contents

To Mark and Steven:
May their memories shine bright.

Chapter One

Beginnings

In the year prior to America's plunge into the "War to end all wars" Oklahoma was stuck in a time "betwixt and between" the modern and post-modern era. While the majority of the citizens who resided in the state's major metropolitan areas readily adapted to the wonders of early twentieth century technology, such as electricity, automobiles, indoor plumbing, and telephones, many residents of the rural heartland still clung to their simple agrarian roots. Daily life in small town Oklahoma was one of endless toil, outhouses, kerosene lamps, homemade clothes, and boredom. The horseless carriage was a novelty seldom seen on the unimproved dirt roads of the hinterlands. The horse and buggy was still a common sight.

For many residents of the one-time Indian Territory the memories of frontier times remained vivid. The decade old state was still flavored by a touch of the old west. The rugged individualist was deeply admired and a self made man was considered the top of the food chain. Northern and Western Oklahoma offered up vast unpopulated prairies stretching as far as the eye could see. Cowboying was still a common occupation practiced at any number of mammoth sized ranches located throughout the state. Many citizens still carried guns on their person and knew how to use them. Horse thieves were often times hung to the nearest tree when apprehended and it was considered acceptable behavior by many to shoot anyone caught cheating at cards.

It was during this time frame that a ruthless band of desperadoes known as the Poe-Hart Gang began their deprivations throughout the width and breadth of Oklahoma. The gang was the first major group of western bank robbers to make the switch from horse to automobile, allowing them to flee the scene of their crimes at what seemed in those days as lightning speed, leaving nothing but trails of gas fumes and dust to tell the tale. Although an active gang only a few months, their daring attacks on Oklahoma's banks and Wild West style shoot-outs with lawmen and vigilantes spread fear and panic across the plains and hills of Eastern and Central Oklahoma. Bold headlines blazed across the front pages of mid-western newspapers noting their activities, reminding folks of the Doolin-Dalton threat of two decades past. Hundreds of citizens joined posses from one end of the state to the other, trying to collect the massive rewards offered "dead or alive" for the gang member's heads on a pole.

Although the gang achieved little fame beyond the Midwest, they were a phenomena of history, a bridge between the old west of Jessie James and that of the more modern depression era gangsters like "Pretty Boy" Floyd. Although historians have often times credited desperadoes Henry Starr and Al Spencer as the inventors of the modern automobile powered bank raid, the reader will learn they were merely emulating the earlier efforts of the Poe-Hart Gang.

Any telling of the history of the Gang and their brief reign of terror must begin with the roots of the men involved. The early development of the gang starts with the Poes, a family whose ancestry and lives have until recently been a mystery.

The original leader and brains of the notorious outfit was a secretive character named Adolphus Lane Poe, who was destined to be known as "Poem", "Pone," or "Pony" Poe, (so named for his love of horse flesh). Poe was born on May 6, 1876, near Webberville in Travis County, Texas. He was the son of William Martin and Nancy Levina Poe, who had immigrated from Tennessee and Arkansas, to the "Lone Star" state in 1872, looking for cheap land and opportunities. The family, made up of the parents, along with a passel of kids, seven boys and three girls, originally settled near the small community of Honey Grove in Fannin County. When a nearby river overflowed, flooding their newly established homestead, the family relocated to a farm fourteen miles south of the capital city of Austin. In 1877, when Adolphus was a year old, they moved to Clay County, Texas, near modern day Henrietta, in the northeast section of the state. In 1882, a cholera outbreak hit the area, bringing death and misery to many of the residents. The Poe family was not spared in the disaster. The father, William, and his wife, Nancy, along with a son John and daughter Martha perished in the epidemic. According to family tradition, the surviving infant children, including young Adolphus were taken in and raised by a series of neighbors and relatives.

At the time of the catastrophe, three of the brothers, Cisero, Bill, and James were grown and on their own. It appears Cisero was employed as a stock wrangler at a nearby ranch, while Bill was punching cattle up the Chisholm Trail. James lived with his wife and children in Hamilton County, south of Fort Worth, where he was a Deputy Sheriff.

In 1886, James Poe was murdered less than a hundred yards from his doorstep. Apparently, the lawman had became card-playing buddies at the local gin mill with a desperate character named Bill Payne, who was rumored to be the head of a cattle rustling enterprise operating in the district. When the grand jury indicted his friend for larceny, the deputy faced an obvious dilemma. The day after the indictment was handed down, Payne spent the night at Poe's home playing cards and nipping on a jug. There are two versions of what happened next. One account suggests Poe spent the evening quarrelling with his friend over whether he should turn himself into the court. Another implies the pair wiled away the hours auguring over their ill-gotten gains (this account suggests the pair were in cahoots in the rustling business).

Regardless of which characterization is true, the end result was the same. The following morning, Poe and his buddy saddled up and began riding towards town. A few

James Dudley Poe, Hamilton County, Texas,
Courtesy of Nelda Poe Smith

minutes later Poe rushed back to his house retrieving a pistol before remounting his horse and resuming his journey. A short time later, Poe's wife, hearing a shot, ran to investigate. She discovered her husband's lifeless form sprawled on the ground with a bullet lodged in his back. A coroner was called to the scene of the crime (county records say he was paid five dollars by the taxpayers for his services). After a brief

The streets of Hamilton, Texas, circa early 1900s. Courtesy, Hamilton County Genealogy Society

investigation, Poe's death was officially ruled a homicide.

Although, Bill Payne was arrested, tried and convicted of Poe's murder, the Texas Court of Appeals overturned the verdict. In 1898, Payne killed a man in a bar fight in Hamilton. He was convicted of manslaughter and sentenced to two years at the Texas State Penitentiary in Huntsville. This time the verdict stuck, and the bad man served his time. Fifteen years later, the gunman's decomposing body was found by a hiker lying on the edge of a pasture near Sayre, Oklahoma. He had been shot in the heart from long range. Many folks at the time believed the Poes had gotten their revenge.

In 1889, the remaining underage Poe siblings apparently joined an Uncle and several of his children on the big Oklahoma land rush, eventually settling in what would

---

Old Federal jail, Fort Smith, Arkansas. Photo by Naomi Morgan

become modern day Canadian County.

By the early 1890s, Adolphus, (we'll call "Pony" from now on for the sake of clarity) after enduring an unsettling childhood, which included being orphaned at the tender a age six and working full-time as a farmhand since age twelve, decided to make his own way in the world. He quickly landed a job as a cowhand on a ranch near the small village of Cheek, which was located in the Chickasaw Nation. Apparently, the hard knock life of a cowboy didn't appeal to the young man. He soon began casting around for an easier way to make ends meet.

Judge Parker's courtroom. Courtesy of Arkansas Historical Society

In the summer of 1894, he and his brother, Bill, stole a herd of horses near Fort Supply, Indian Territory; Pony was promptly caught, convicted and sentenced to three years in the Federal Penitentiary. Bill evaded justice for nearly a year before a Federal Marshal apprehended him in the Sansbois Mountains deep in the Choctaw Nation. The accused thief was transported to the Federal Jail in Fort Smith, Arkansas where the daunting Isaac C. Parker, the so-called "Hanging Judge" held court. Serving on the bench for nearly a quarter century, the Judge, whose jurisdiction included both the Indian Territory and the Western District of Arkansas, had condemned 79 men to the gallows, located just south and east of his courtroom. When Poe's case finally came to court, the good Judge saw fit to sentence the thirty nine year old thief to a term of six years in the Federal lockup.

With good behavior, Pony was released from prison in the winter of 1897. He again took up residence near Cheek, where he made the acquaintance of a young woman by the name of Elizabeth (Lizzie) Dotson, the daughter of Texas immigrants. A Justice of the Peace married the couple on January 20, 1898 in Cheek. The pair settled down just outside the small village and was soon blessed with the

Ranch scene, circa 1900. Courtesy Okmulgee Public Library

birth of a daughter, Annie Lee. The following year, Pony's five-year-old nephew, Johnny Ferrell, moved in with the couple. No one seems to know why the lad took up residence with his Aunt and Uncle, but he stayed on until he was grown.

But alas, domestic bliss doesn't always guarantee success when it comes to changing the stripes on a polecat. In 1902, Pony, was arrested for his suspected involvement with a band of stock thieves who had recently conducted a

Site of the Poe Cabin near Nuyaka Mission as it is today. Photo by R. D. Morgan

Nuyaka Creek Boarding School, circa 1920.
Courtesy Okmulgee Public Library

series of raids on several large isolated ranches in south central Oklahoma. Whether brother Bill, who had recently been released from prison, was part of the horse theft ring is unknown. It appears that a few weeks after his arrest, the case against Pony was dropped for lack of evidence.

Sometime around 1903, Pony, (he seems to have taken this name permanently by 1900, where he is listed as Pone Poe on U. S. census records) moved his family to the small settlement of Nuyaka (originally named Hance settlement) in the Creek Indian Nation, twelve miles northwest of present day Okmulgee, Oklahoma.

Poe settled near the old Nuyaka Indian Mission renting a small cabin and a few acres of pastureland from a local Indian who operated a nearby sawmill. By this time, his family was made up of his wife, Lizzie, her widowed mother, along with a son; age three, a five-year-old daughter and Pony's nine-year-old nephew, Johnny. For the next few years, the family raised hogs and cotton, ranched, and occasionally dealt in stolen stock for their survival.

In 1904, Bill Poe was arrested for armed robbery near

Prison guards at McAlester circa 1915 Courtesy of The Oklahoma Department of Corrections

the town of Ardmore, Chickasaw Nation. This time, the law lowered the boom on the outlaw, handing him a fifteen-year sentence. Soon after his conviction, Bill's wife

"Big Mac" Courtesy of the Oklahoma Department of Corrections.

Okfuskee County Sheriff Will McCulley (right side, white shirt) with Deputy and prisoners, circa 1909. Courtesy Okfuskee County Historical museum.

abandoned their thirteen-year-old son, Oscar, on Pony's doorstep before taking off to parts unknown.

On taking up residence at Nuyaka, Poe's children and nephews were offered the opportunity to live a carefree, "Tom Sawyer" like existence, in a setting filled with pure adventure and the best that Mother Nature had to offer. Nuyaka in the early 1900s was a small backwoods village virtually untouched by civilization. The nearby Deep Fork River bottoms was a wild, pristine wilderness, heavily populated with deer, bear, and wild turkey. If taken the notion, a young boy could have wandered the country for miles without seeing a soul.

Although the other children in the family seemed to have adjusted well to their new environment, one of the kids, Oscar, evolved into a deeply troubled lad. He was reportedly infected by the family's darker impulses, rampaging through the area stealing and vandalizing at will. Unfortunately, his uncle involved him in his horse thieving activities by the time he was old enough to ride. In 1908, at the age of seventeen he was arrested along with several other boys for stealing a herd of ten blooded horses from a nearby ranch. Okfuskee County Sheriff Will McCulley tossed the young man into a cell in the County Jail in Okemah, where he left him to his own devices for a few days to ponder on his predicament before offering him an opportunity to gain his freedom by returning the livestock to their rightful owners. Over the next week, the Sheriff, with Oscar's aid recovered eight of the ten horses. For his assistance, McCulley let the teen off the hook, dropping the charges with a stern warning that another theft and he'd be heading for the newly built state prison in McAlester.

In the fall of 1909, McCulley again arrested Oscar for horse theft, which was a very serious crime in those days. In 1909, the world was truly horse driven. To steal a man's horse was to deprive him of a way of making a living as well as his basic transportation. McCulley kept his word; Oscar was convicted of Grand Larceny and given a two-year stretch at the state rock pile to rethink the direction his life had taken. He didn't learn a thing.

In the months following Oscar's release from prison, he was suspected of participating in four incidents of horse theft in Okmulgee and Okfuskee Counties. The slippery young thief managed to stay out of the clutches of the law until October of 1912 when he was arrested in Garvin County, Oklahoma, for horse rustling. This time the judge sentenced him to five years in the state pen. After serving a year in "Big Mac," as the penitentiary in McAlester was dubbed, Oscar was transferred to the Granite Reformatory in Western Oklahoma to finish his term. While at Granite, he was made a trustee and assigned as a dog handler to Assistant Warden W. O. Green's team of guards and trustees whose job it was to capture escaped prisoners. The Warden stated Poe was a great asset to prison officials in tracking down cons who had "taken to the bush." Green, who had taken a shine to the young man, helped him obtain a provisional parole in the winter of 1915.

No. 64		**OSR**
NAME Oscar Poe	COLOR White	AGE
SENTENCE BEGINS 3-11-10	TERM 2 yrs.	
CRIME Grand Larceny	COUNTY Okfuskee	

DISCHARGED   12-10-11

Oscar Poe, Oklahoma prison record. OSP.

Chapter Two

Horse Thieves

After his discharge from prison, Oscar, who authorities, relatives and news reports described as a generally well dressed, handsome man, with a keen sense of humor and the morals of an alley cat, sought out honest work as a freight hauler in the then booming oil fields around Drumright, Oklahoma. His efforts at clean living appear to have been short lived. After a month on the job, he stole a mule team and wagon that had been placed in his care. Driving the rig to nearby Seminole, he attempted to sell the outfit to another oil company. A company representative, becoming wary of the brash young man, immediately contacted authorities with his suspicions. A trap was set by lawmen to capture the up and coming young outlaw and retrieve the mules. When a pair of officers attempted to arrest Poe later that night, a gunfight ensued resulting

Oil field in Central Oklahoma circa 1920.
Courtesy of the Seminole Public Library

in both officers being gravely wounded. Poe hastily fled the area minus the stolen mules. Unfortunately, for Oscar, he was recognized and a warrant was put out for his arrest on a charge of attempted murder and grand larceny. After the Seminole fiasco, Poe fled to his Uncle Pony's secluded Nuyaka ranch to lay low for a spell.

It is here at Pony's ranch where he apparently encountered his future partners in crime, the Hart brothers, William and Harrison. The twins were born in September 1894 in Labette County, Kansas, the sons of George Washington Hart, an immigrant from England, and Nora Heldenbrand Hart, the offspring of Illinois immigrants. A few years after the twin's birth, the Harts moved from Kansas to the little Northeast Oklahoma village of Centralia, located midway between the towns of Nowata and Vinita. The marriage produced a total of eight children, six boys and two girls. The father died prematurely of a heart attack while working as a laborer at the nearby settlement of Pyramid Corners leaving the family rudderless and poverty stricken.

Downtown Drumright, Oklahoma circa 1914. Courtesy of The Drumright Oil Field Museum

Papa Hart's untimely death left a widow alone to raise eight kids. She apparently had little control over her growing children. The boys soon gained a reputation in Centralia as young hellions, stealing anything that wasn't chained down in the little village. But as much as the local merchants complained, the poor mother was apparently incapable of gaining even the smallest semblance of supervision over her lads. The twins were soon accused of burglarizing a local business among other depravations. In 1915, William, or Will as he was called, shot and wounded John Hale, a schoolteacher at nearby Big Creek, who had allegedly scolded his sister Nori for getting out of line in the classroom. Fearing arrest, he and his twin brother Harry, fled the area riding a southbound freight.

There are numerous versions of how the Hart boys made the acquaintance of Pony Poe. Several area historians have placed the twins in contact with the old thief by way of their being the elder Poe's grandsons. Another tale names the pair as Oscar Poe's nephews by marriage. But according to modern day Poe and Hart family descendents, census reports, genealogy texts, and other existing public and private records there is no known connection relating the two families either through blood or marriage. The best evidence seems to indicate that after fleeing the Osage

Cowboys on the Oklahoma plains. Courtesy Okmulgee Public Library

Country, the boys made their way to Muskogee, Oklahoma, where they first encountered Pony Poe who had entered his blooded horses in the annual races at the fairgrounds. The Hart twins, being of slight build and having worked as jockeys in numerous races back home, were hired by the older man to ride his steeds. When the fair ended, the wayward youths, who had apparently been practicing the age old art of pick pocketing, as well as jack rolling drunks on the city's north side for eating and "walking around" money since arriving in town, accompanied Poe to his ranch near Nuyaka. It's likely that at this time the pair was recruited into Poe's prolific horse theft ring.

By the winter of 1915 and into 1916, good horse flesh had become a precious commodity. After the outbreak of WWI, European nations began fielding huge, mainly horse driven armies on the killing fields of the continent. They quickly began sending livestock buyers to the American West offering top dollar for nags, which had previously

Soldiers at Fort Sumner New Mexico circa 1890s. Courtesy of New Mexico Historical Society

fetched five dollars at the local glue factory.

A further tightening in the horse market occurred in 1916 when the Civil War that was taking place in Mexico spilled over the border onto American soil. When the Mexican outlaw Poncho Villa led a contingent of irregular Calvary raiding the small town of Columbus, New Mexico, the American response was to begin a massive buildup of troops on the US-Mexican border. Shortly afterward, General John J. Pershing commanded an expeditionary force of nearly 20,000 men, made up of mostly Calvary and horse pulled artillery units in pursuit of Villa's guerrilla contingent deep into northern Mexico. Horse and mule buying stations were set up by Pershing at Forts Reno, Oklahoma, and Sumner in New Mexico. The Muskogee Times-Democrat reported in the October 19, 1916 issue, government buyers at Fort Scott, Kansas were paying up to $200 for anything with four legs and the strength to pull a wagon. Government stock buyers, becoming involved in heated competition with foreign purchase agents, didn't seem to care where the hay burners came from or whether they were stolen or not.

For a man like Pony Poe, who had been a practicing horse thief since his teens, these circumstances made for a veritable bonanza. He and his small crew couldn't steal enough horses to satisfy the demand. He quickly decided to expand his business and hire more personnel to meet the bull market. From all indications, the rustling operation the elder Poe devised, was divided into several stages. First, Oscar and his crew would fan out into the countryside. When they came upon an unattended herd of horses, they would wait until nightfall, then under the cover of darkness herd the ponies to an isolated canyon located near Pony's Nuyaka ranch. Once the stock was corralled, the elder Poe along with Harry Hart and probably Johnny

Ferrell, would sort and re-brand the horses before driving them west to be sold to either ranchers or the military.

Around this time, Oscar and his new found friend, Will Hart, traveled back to the Hart's old haunts in the Northeast section of the state, an area dotted with large ranching operations flush with horse flesh, to engage in horse thieving raids there and across the nearby Kansas border. Not long after their arrival in mid-December, a posse led by Nowata County Sheriff James Mayes captured the pair in possession of a herd of freshly stolen horses. Oscar, going by the alias of "Mack Roe," and Will Hart were promptly lodged in the Nowata County jail where they made the acquaintance of a pair of local neer-do-wells named Jess Littrell and Thomas "Russell" Tucker. Poe recruited the pair, who was presently incarcerated on bootlegging charges, into his horse-thieving ring. Apparently, it was decided since both Littrell and Tucker knew the area and Poe had the connections for getting rid of the stock, it was a match made in heaven. The pairing would soon become a match made in hell for area ranchers and businessmen.

One of Oscar's new recruits was an old hand in the

Photo of Oscar Poe and Will Hart taken at the time of their arrest in Coffeyville, Kansas. Courtesy of the Muskogee Phoenix

Russell Tucker circa 1915. Courtesy of Joe Tucker

larceny business; he'd ridden the veritable "Hoot Owl Trail" for many years. Jess Littrell was born in Texas in September of 1884. In the early 1890s, his family moved across the Red River taking up residence in the Indian Territory. Little is known of his early life, but records show he and another man stole a herd of horses in Arkansas shortly after the turn of the century, but the pair was quickly tracked down and arrested by Deputy US Marshal Tom Burk in Oklahoma's Arbuckle Moun-

Nowata County Sheriff James Mayes. Courtesy Nowata County Historical Society

tains. Littrell, described by police reports as 5' 10", and blue eyes, with raven black hair, which he parted in the middle, was convicted of the crime, and served two years in Federal Prison. After his release, he traveled to Bartlesville, Oklahoma, in the north-central section of the state where he took a job as a freighter. Like Oscar Poe, his stab at honest employment was short lived and he soon became involved in the bootlegging business, selling home-made rotgut whiskey to the "roughnecks" working in the

Nowata County Court House with the jail located in the basement. Courtesy of the Nowata County Historical Society

booming Osage oil patch. While conducting business in nearby Coffeyville, Kansas, Littrell met and married a woman who operated the Rex Boarding house, located in the downtown Upman block. Apparently, it was not a happy coupling. She promptly divorced him after his being thrown in jail a time or two. Although the couple continued to "keep company," they apparently never lived together after the divorce.

According to Nowata County Court records, in June of 1911, Littrell was arrested and jailed on a transporting ardent spirits charge. After serving a six-month stint in the county jail, he was released, but did not learn his lesson. Records indicate he was rearrested on the same charge in both Ponca City in 1912 and Pawhuska in 1913.

Evidently, he made the acquaintance of his future partner in crime, Russell Tucker, on the saloon lined streets of South Coffeyville. Unlike most of his fellow gang members, the Missouri born Tucker was by all accounts a product of a good home. Nicknamed "Little One," his fall from grace was apparently due to his addiction to strong drink and poor choice of companions. In September of 1915, he and Littrell, who were by then full time partners in the moonshine business, were jailed on a whiskey selling charge (possession of five gallons of homemade liquor) in Nowata County. The duo bonded out in January 1916. Within a month of his release, Tucker was once more arrested on a separate bootlegging offense. He quickly made bail and rejoined his sidekick, who had partnered up full time with Poe and his faithful minion, Will Hart, in their horse-rustling venture.

The spring of 1916 was a time of great success for the gang. The huge sprawling unfenced ranches in the area were bursting at the seams with livestock, offering easy pickings for the ordinary horse thief. After meeting with such prosperity, the gang was soon forced to begin recruiting additional outside help. Their first batch of recruits included a quartet of local boys, Lee Jarrett, his brothers Glenn and Floyd along with their brother-in-law, Albert "Ab" Connor. These men were all well known to authorities, having been arrested and charged with a host of crimes over the years, which included transporting illegal spirits, robbery, and larceny.

The Jarrett brothers came from a notorious family of wrongdoers originally hailing from St. Joseph, Missouri.

Of ten brothers, seven went on to be career criminals. On March 31, 1911, Walter, the eldest, along with brothers Lee and Glenn joined with Ab Connor, and a small time crook named Elmer McCurdy, in robbing the Iron Mountain Railroad at Lenapah, Oklahoma. When the bandits blasted the train's safe with nitro, they apparently calculated incorrectly how much of the potent substance to use. The explosion blew the contents of the strongbox into a nearby

Floyd Jarrett. Courtesy of Master Detective.

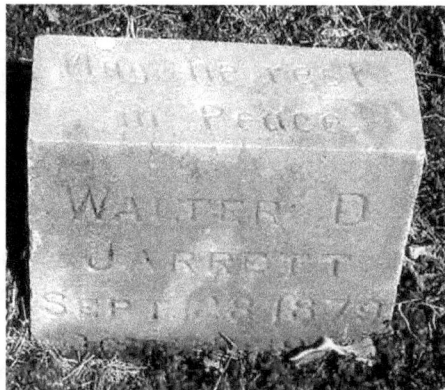

Grave of Walter Jarrett, Ball Cemetery. Photo by Naomi Morgan

cotton field. Soon after the failed train robbery, a posse tracked two of the bandits directly to the Jarrett farm, six miles east of town. At the residence, authorities found a case of dynamite, a box of blasting caps, and a bottle of nitroglycerin. Also recovered at the scene were several rifles, identified as those stolen in a recent burglary of a hardware store in nearby Centralia. Glenn Jarrett and Connor were promptly arrested on the burglary charge and transported to the Craig County Jail for safekeeping. Federal authorities put a hold on the pair for suspicion of involvement in the Lenapah train robbery. Several months later, brothers Lee and Walter were arrested in Lenapah while visiting Lee's home, where he lived with his wife and three children when not on the scout from the law. Both men were transported to the Federal lockup in Muskogee to be tried for the train robbery. Shortly thereafter, Lee was released for lack of evidence but Walter was tried and convicted of the railroad heist.

On May 15, 1912, Walter and four others sawed through the bars of their cell in the Muskogee jail fleeing into the night. Five months later, on the morning of October 12, 1912, Walter, single handedly robbed the bank of Prue, Oklahoma, at gunpoint. Later that evening, a local rancher named Burke and a friend met the desperado riding across the prairie between Prue and Tulsa. When the pair noticed the mount Walter was riding matched the description and brand of a horse stolen the previous night from an area rancher, they began to question him about the legal ownership of the pony. Answering pointed questions not being one of Walter's strong suits, the fugitive pulled his six-shooter and started throwing lead at his interrogators. In the ensuing gunfight, Walter killed the horse one of his antagonists was riding, but lost his own life in the process. So much for Walter.

While big brother was learning his lesson in "crime doesn't pay," younger brother Glenn and his pal, Ab Connor, was sweating it out in the Nowata County Jail. Authorities weren't getting a pair of virgins when they apprehended Jarrett and Connor; both had been incarcerated on numerous occasions over the years. Glenn Jarrett had a particularly lengthy criminal record being first arrested in 1911 on a charge of horse theft. His criminal resume also included charges of grand larceny in 1912, selling intoxicating spirits in 1913, another horse theft in the same year, as well as a burglary charge for which he was sentenced to a five-year jolt in the Kansas State Prison. He would later be indicted for an auto theft along with an aggravated assault in Nowata County. Albert Connor, who incidentally was a double in-law to the Jarretts, (he was not only married to their sister Hazel, but his own sister was married to Lee Jarrett), didn't have quite as lengthy of record, but his life had followed the same basic pattern as his partner.

In March 1916, the Nowata County grand jury indicted Poe and Hart on the horse theft charge, as well as Tucker and Littrell on their bootlegging counts. The bonds of all four men were revoked due to their suspected involvement in various crimes while on bail. Naturally, none of the four surrendered to authorities, preferring to jump bail and go on the scout. Around this time, Oscar Poe and his buddy, Will Hart, apparently made their residence in nearby Independence, Kansas, while operating their criminal enterprises south of the border. For companionship, the boys shacked up with a pair of females they had supposedly met at a local "Sportin' House." Hart with a Helen Wieman and Oscar with a cute brunette named Mabel Brooks. Authorities characterized the two "ladies" as lewd

The square, Coffeyville Kansas. Isham Hardware right center. Courtesy Coffeyville Public Library

Ninth street Coffeyville, Kansas, circa early 1900s. Courtesy of the Kansas Historical Society

Advertisement Isham Hardware in a 1917 issue of the Coffeyville Daily Journal. Courtesy of The Coffeyville Daily Journal

The Isham Hdw. Co.

A Few Other Suggestions:

Foot Ball
Basket Ball
Boxing Gloves
Base Ball and Bat
Tennis Racket
Gun
Punching Bag
Sleds
Wagon
Wheel Barrows
Bicycle
Tricycles.

FREE
A
Return Ring
Kite
for the asking.
Worth
the
While
wd think.

The Isham Hdw. Co.

women, or gals who had "seen a lot of moonlight in their time."

Meanwhile, area farmers and ranchers began losing an amazing amount of stock. Anti-Horse thief Organizations began cropping up in Craig and Nowata counties. Several horse thieves were tracked down in the area and left hanging in trees as an example to those contemplating horse rustling as a career choice. Authorities at this time had only a vague idea of who was behind the sudden outbreak of stock thefts.

The rustling ring, now made up of Pony Poe, his nephew Oscar, along with the Harts, Littrell, Tucker, Lee, Glenn, and Floyd Jarrett, Albert Connor, Red Cloud Scruggs, and probably Johnny Ferrell, kept up their depravations for the majority of 1916. In the fall of that year, several members of the gang branched out into nighttime burglaries of numerous small country stores throughout Nowata and Craig Counties. When the band robbed the Reverend Billy Barr's small store near Childers, Oklahoma, they left a note thanking him for the money and supplies. As time went by, the gang slowly switched from burglary and horse theft, to a much bolder activity, armed robbery.

On October 2, at about 2 a. m., three well-dressed men suspected to have been Oscar Poe, Will Hart, and Jess Littrell walked into the office of the Metropolitan Hotel in Coffeyville, Kansas armed with Colt .45 automatic pistols. The trio encountered a black porter named Bill Mathews, who when ordered to raise his hands reacted by bolting down a nearby hallway, jumping out an open window. After this unexpected development, the intruders walked behind the office counter and rifled the contents of the hotel's cash register, which yielded a whopping ten dollars. A guest, who innocently walked into the office, was also stuck up. A search of his person turned up a single five-cent piece. He was told to keep it and buy a cigar. The bandits then pounded on the door of the manager's private living quarters. The hotel's proprietor, a Mrs. Josie Dunkerton, opened her door angrily demanding an explanation to this interruption of her early morning slumbers. The gang's leader, Oscar Poe, asked her forgiveness for waking her, but explained he was robbing the hotel and could not locate where the hostelry kept their big money. The woman refused to cooperate, so the outlaws shook her down finding a large roll of bills hidden in her bloomers. The thieves then casually strolled out the front door, disappearing into the night.

When interviewed by the police, who arrived a few minutes after the robbery, the manager stated the gang's leader, whom she described as a "dandy," had visited the hotel earlier that evening inquiring about the price of a room, than abruptly left without a word. The following day, police issued a statement claiming the three bandits matched the descriptions of a similar trio who had robbed Coffeyville's Iron Mountain Inn the previous week for $350 in cash and coin.

Less than a week later, on October 8, at one in the morning, Coffeyville Patrolman Lister Handy and Merchant Patrolman Fred Wanenwetsh noticed four men loitering in front of the Condon Bank on the town's square. The officers reportedly shadowed the men for an hour until the suspicious quartet faded away. The pair of officers parted company around 3 a. m. Handy telling his fellow officer he was going back to the police station after he checked out the alley behind the nearby Isham Hardware store.

As Handy neared the rear of the building, he saw a shadow. He turned on his flashlight. Suddenly, the same four characters he had earlier observed loafing on the square surrounded him. The men, all pointing pistols at the unlucky officer relieved him of his gun, flashlight, and badge, even the brass buttons on his coat. One of the robbers, who authorities suspected to have been Oscar Poe, told the hapless lawman to "take hold of this sack, boy." He was then forced to help the men haul an incredible amount of stolen items from the hardware store to the thieves' car parked two blocks away. After the robbers had collected all the plunder they could fit in the automobile, they forced Handy to strip down to his BVDs, tying him to a nearby telephone pole. As Poe attempted to stuff one of his soiled socks into his mouth as a gag, Handy asked if his clean handkerchief wouldn't do just as well. The thieves chuckled, but agreed to his logical proposal. After a great deal of effort, the poor officer was able to dislodge the gag and immediately began screaming bloody murder. The proprietor and several boarders at the nearby Miller Hotel heard the struggling cop and released the humiliated man. His shoes and clothes were found the following day in a trash can on the edge of town.

A general alarm was sent out to surrounding communities. Several large posses were formed and spent the remainder of night and the following day running patrols and manning roadblocks throughout the area hoping to catch sight of the slippery bandits. The take from the bold burglary was a bulging carload of rifles, shotguns, pistols, straight razors, watches, ammunition, and hunting apparel. The authorities later identified the four burglars as Oscar Poe(alais Mack Roe), Jess Littrell, Will Hart, and Russell Tucker. When the Chief of Police was interviewed the following day, he assured reporters and the public the desperadoes, whom he suspected had used at least two cars in their previous nights robbery, would soon be in police custody. The top cop also claimed the perpetrators in all three recent robberies were the same individuals.

The gang, feeling they were pressing their luck in Coffeyville, moved their operations to Oklahoma where on the evening of October 16, the same four characters pounced on a unsuspecting dance hall resort named the

First National Bank of Centralia, Oklahoma, circa 1930s. Courtesy of the Craig County Historical Society.

Centralia today, a modern day ghost town. Bank was located near grove of trees. Photo by Naomi Morgan

"Tin Pan," located on Nowata's east side. The bandits tapped the till for about $1,000 before relieving guests in the packed honky-tonk of their valuables to the tune of over $500 in cash, and a King's ransom in watches, jewelry, and other valuables. During the robbery, Nowata Policeman Al May, unaware a stickup was taking place, strolled into the nightclub, where he immediately had a pistol jammed into his ribs and told gruffly to "pony up, cowboy." The bandits stole the poor officer's gun, badge, hat, and gold watch. When the club's manager, Mrs. Eva Howard, begun loudly protesting the treatment of her patrons, she was firmly told to "shut your yap, missy" by the gang's leader. Nowata Police stated the robbers escaped in a high-powered automobile, heading east.

The band of hooligans then turned their greedy eyes toward the small isolated town of Centralia, located eighteen miles northwest of Vinita, Oklahoma. The village, which was built around a public square, hosted a bevy of businesses. Located on the southwest corner of the square was the First National Bank owned by the Montgomery brothers, a wealthy family of area ranchers. The bank, chartered in 1909, had never been robbed and was the pride of the little berg, a constant reminder to the towns folk of the area's economic health. The settlement was also the hometown of the Hart brothers.

At about noon on October 18, four men drove up in a high-powered Ford touring car parking directly in front of the bank's front door. Three men piled out of the car entering the building, while another man, his face painted pitch black, stayed at the wheel of the running auto. Going about their business inside the institution was the bank's officers Henry, Claud, and T. R. Montgomery, who was also president of the institution, along with C. C. Worrall, a Centralia merchant. Also present was Bank Teller Fred

Hartley and John Wise the President of the Farmers State Bank of Vinita, who had unluckily chosen this day to visit his friends, the Montgomerys.

According to statements made to the press after the event, the bankers noticed nothing unusual until three bandits suddenly came bursting through the front door hollering, "This is a holdup, get down on the floor." The employees complied, lying on the marble floor with hands outstretched. Hartley, the cashier was instructed to get up and let the thieves into the bank vault. The lead bandit reportedly held a cocked gun against the badly frightened teller's head while he nervously worked the vault's combination. The outlaws gathered up about $5,000 in cash and coin from the bank's coffers. Another hundred dollars, several pocket watches, and a handful of jewelry were collected from the crowd of employees and witnesses. Bank President T. R. Montgomery later claimed the bandits had cleaned out the institution so thoroughly, "not one thin dime could be found in the bank or on any of the witnesses' person after the affair, they even stole the clock off the wall." The trio then calmly walked to the front door and bid their victims farewell. Their fleeing car was seen heading west out of town at a slow and even pace by witnesses in the street. An area merchant named Grimes, suspecting something was amiss, peered into the bankís front window and then turned and bolted into the street screaming, "the bank is robbed" at the top of his lungs.

Ironically, just sitting down to their noon meal in a cafè located about a hundred yards from the bank's front door, was County Sheriff M. B. Lionberger, Deputy Federal Marshal L. P. Smart, and Deputy Sheriff Lee Webb. They were having a conference planning a strategy to cut down on thefts in the area. When the alarm was given the embarrassed lawmen quickly gathered a posse and set out in four cars heading west in pursuit of the bold bandits. Near the small village of Rudy, several witnesses sighted the bandit's fleeing car. They described the occupants as three men dressed as women and a fourth man disguised as a Negro; his face was covered in shoe polish or a black cork substance. It was a bizarre identification.

Later that afternoon, the same band of brigands held up the small village store at nearby Coodys Bluff at gunpoint. Lawmen throughout the northeast section of the state were notified and numerous posses swarmed the area, but after scouring the region for several days, the vigilantes gave up returning to their homes and businesses in disgust. The robbers of the Centralia and Coodys Bluff store were later identified as Oscar Poe (alias Mack Roe), Will Hart, and Jess Littrell with either Russell Tucker or Lee Jarrett driving the getaway vehicle.

THE STATE OF OKLAHOMA

vs.

Russel Tucker

Defendant.

In the .... County .... Court

of .... Nowata .... County, Oklahoma

IN THE NAME AND BY THE AUTHORITY OF THE STATE OF OKLAHOMA

Now comes .... C. W. Mason .... the duly qualified and acting County Attorney,

in and for .... Nowata .... County, State of Oklahoma, and gives the ... said County ....

Court of .... Nowata .... County, State of Oklahoma, to know and be informed that

.... Russel Tucker ....

did, in .... Nowata .... County, and in the State of Oklahoma, on or about the ... 23rd ....

day of .... September .... in the year of our Lord One Thousand Nine Hundred and ...... Sixteen ......

and anterior to the presentment hereof, commit the crime of ....

.... Carrying Concealed Weapons ....

in the manner and form as follows, to-wit: ... That the said Russel Tucker then and there being

... did then and there, intentionally and unlawfully and wilfully carry ......

..... concealed on and about his person a pistol, towit a weapon ....

NAMES OF WITNESSES

Henry Hutchison

N. Couch

Russell Tucker, carrying concealed weapon charge, Nowata County.

NO. 8572 OSP

NAME Jess Littrell COLOR W AGE
SENTENCE BEGINS 11-26-17 TERM Life
CRIME Murder COUNTY Okfuskee

Also 25 years for conjoint robbery in Oklahoma Co;

With Ref, 4-3-28

Released under guard to Nowata County for tria
per order of Governor 9-3-29
Returned 9-9-29
Released to C. I. Bureau officers to be trans
ferred to Nowata for trial 10-15-29 over

Jess Littrell - Okalhoma prison record, OSP.

Returned from Nowata Trial 10-19-29

Discharged 10-11-29

Prison record - OSP.

No. 21216 8572

Name Jess Littrell OSP Color W Age 45
Sentence begins 10-11-29 Term Life
Crime Murder County Okfuskee

old # 8572

12-17-30, discharged on 21216 & rebeled
on his old number 8572
Paroled 7-17-31 for 12 months.
Permanent Parole granted 7-8-32
Pardon granted 11-5-34.

Prison record - OSP.

Nowata County court record – bootlegging charge.

Lee Jarrett – bootlegging charge, Nowata County.

Tucker and Littrell Nowata County court record.

Jess Littrell – bootlegging – 1912, Nowata County.

Bail document – Lee Jarrett, Nowata County.

THE STATE OF OKLAHOMA,

To the Sheriff of Nowata County

WHEREAS, Complaint in writing, and upon oath has been filed in the County Court of Nowata County, charging that Glen Jarrett, John Harrington and Ed Walsh

did on or about the 22d day of November 1912, in the County of Nowata, State of Oklahoma, commit the crime of Larceny in the dwelling house of Albert Fisher by stealing and carrying away the following, to-wit: One ladies gold watch value $25.00, one No. 12 Britch loading shot gun value $18.00; one pair cissors value .75, six silver plated knives and six silver plated forks value $4.00, total value $47.75, the same being the property of Albert Fisher.

You are therefore commanded forthwith to take said Glenn Jarrett, John Harrington, Ed Welch and bring him before me or some other magistrate having cognizance of the case to be dealt with according to law.

Given under my hand and the seal of the County Court of said County,

this 24th day of January 1913.

Glenn Jarrett – robbery charges, Nowata County.

THE STATE OF OKLAHOMA,

To the Sheriff of Nowata County

WHEREAS, Complaint in writing, and upon oath has been filed in the County Court of Nowata County, charging that _Glenn Jarrett_ did on or about the _23_ day of _August_ _191 1_, in the County of Nowata, State of Oklahoma, commit the crime of _Larceny by taking bay horse of value $100 lawful money of United States property of George Carter_

You are therefore commanded forthwith to take said _Defendant_ and bring him before me or some other magistrate having cognizance of the case to be dealt with according to law.

Given under my hand and the seal of the County Court of said County, this _2nd_ day of _September_ 191 1

Wm F. Gilruth
County Judge

Glenn Jarrett – horse theft, Nowata County.

THE STATE OF OKLAHOMA,

To the Sheriff of Nowata County

WHEREAS, Complaint in writing, and upon oath has been filed in the County Court of Nowata County, charging that _Glenn Jarrett_ did on or about the _22_ day of _June_ _191 3_, in the County of Nowata, State of Oklahoma, commit the crime of _Unlawful possession of Intoxicating Liquor._

You are therefore commanded forthwith to take said _Glenn Jarrett_ and bring him before me or some other magistrate having cognizance of the case to be dealt with according to law.

Given under my hand and the seal of the County Court of said County, this _24_ day of _June_ 191 3

Wm F. Gilruth
County Judge

Glenn Jarrett – whiskey violation, Nowata County.

INDICTMENT.

STATE OF OKLAHOMA,
Nowata County,

IN DISTRICT COURT.

THE STATE OF OKLAHOMA,

Plaintiff,

No. _____

_____Russell Tucker_____

Defendant

IN THE NAME AND BY THE AUTHORITY OF THE STATE OF OKLAHOMA.

At the ____February____ 19 16 Term of the District Court of Nowata County, State of Oklahoma, begun and held at the City of Nowata, in said County on the _____7th_____ day of ___February____ Nineteen Hundred and _____Sixteen_____ the Grand Jury of said County, good and lawful men, legally drawn and summoned according to law, and then and there examined, impaneled, sworn and charged according to law, to diligently inquire into, and true presentment make, of all public offenses against the State of Oklahoma, committed or triable within said County, upon their said oaths, in the name and by the authority of the State of Oklahoma, do present and find that in said Nowata County, and State of Oklahoma, on the _____ ___2nd___ day of ____March_____ in the year of our Lord One Thousand Nine Hundred and _____Sixteen_____and prior to the finding of this indictment __the above named defendant Russell Tucker_____

did commit the crime of Unlawful Possession of Intoxicating Liquors in the manner and form as follows, towit: the said Russell Tucker then and there being, did then and there unlawfully and wilfully have in his possession certain intoxicating liquor, towit Three ½ pints of whiskey with the wilful and unlawful intent in him, the said Russell Tucker then and there to sell, barter, give away and otherwise dispose of said intoxicating liquor then and there in his possession

contrary to the form of the statutes in such cases made and provided, and against the peace and dignity of the State.

R. M. Millar

~~County Attorney in and for said County~~
Assistant Attorney General

Russell Tucker – bootlegging charge, Nowata County.

THE STATE OF OKLAHOMA

vs.

R. A. Snyder, W. D. McDonough, and Jess Littrell

Defendant

In the _____ County _____ Court
of _____ Nowata _____ County, Oklahoma

IN THE NAME AND BY THE AUTHORITY OF THE STATE OF OKLAHOMA,

Now comes _____ C. W. Mason _____ the duly qualified and acting County Attorney, in and for _____ Nowata _____ County, State of Oklahoma, and gives the said County _____ Court of _____ Nowata _____ County, State of Oklahoma, to know and be informed that _____ R. A. Snyder, W. D. McDonough and Jess Littrell _____

did, in _____ Nowata _____ County, and in the State of Oklahoma, on or about the 27th day of _____ March _____ in the year of our Lord One thousand Nine Hundred and _____ Fifteen _____ and anterior to the presentment hereof, commit the crime of _____ Unlawful possession of intoxicating liquor _____

in the manner and form as follows, to-wit: that the said R. A. Snyder, W. D. McDonough and Jess Littrell, **xxx** then and there being, did then and there unlawfully and wilfully have in their possession intoxicating liquors, towit, 12 quarts of beer and 6 quarts and 1 ½ pint of whiskey, with the wilful and unlawful intention in the said R. A. Snyder, W. D. McDonough and Jess Littrell then and there to sell, barter, give away and otherwise dispose of said intoxicating liquours in their possession

contrary to the form of the statutes, in such cases made and provided, and against the peace and dignity of the State

[signature]
County Attorney.

Jess Littrell and others – bootlegging charges – 1915, Nowata County.

Chapter Three

Stand and Deliver

On October 27, 1916, operatives of the Burn's Detective Agency, employed by the Oklahoma Banker's Association began surveillance of two couples who were living quietly in a small cottage in Independence, Kansas. Through a confidential source, the sleuths had obtained information pointing to the involvement of the two male members of the group in the recent Centralia, Oklahoma, bank robbery. The following day, the quartet mysteriously packed up their belongings, traveling to nearby Coffeyville, Kansas, where they took up residence at a boarding house owned by Doctor and Mrs. T. W. Heuston located at 713 West Eleventh Street.

After observing the suspects for a day, the private detectives contacted the Coffeyville Police Department for assistance. The dicks explained to local authorities, the people under surveillance were most likely the principle actors in the Centralia heist. Coffeyville Police Chief Troutman, along with several other uniformed officers, joined the pair of detectives stationed across the street from the apartment house. Centralia Bankers Claud and Henry Montgomery were contacted and soon showed up on the scene. To the cop's extreme discomfort, a crowd of twenty-five to thirty curious citizens gathered nearby to watch the activities. When one of the male suspects left the house on an errand, the Montgomerys positively identified him as the lead bandit involved in the raid on their bank.

A few minutes past noon, the individual returned. At that point, the police talked some hapless citizen into knocking on the suspect's door to demand their surrender. The lady answering the door greeted the character with a blank stare, listened intently while he gave his spiel, and then abruptly slammed the door in his face fleeing inside. For the next five hours, authorities attempted to coax the culprits into surrendering. Finally, about 5:30 P.M.. two men and two women walked out the front entrance of the building with their hands up. They identified themselves as Mack and Mabel Roe, Will Hart, and Helen Curry. The bevy of suspects were arrested and placed in separate cells at the city jail.

Back at the residence, a thorough search uncovered a leather pouch engraved with gold writing stating it was the property of the First National Bank of Centralia. Concealed inside the pouch was about fifty dollars in paper money. Also found lying in a bathtub filled with water was a large burlap bag wrapped in a soaking wet wool horse blanket. The bag contained several rolls of cash, a bag of gold coins, and a pistol, which turned out to be the property of Policeman Al May, who had been relieved of the six-shooter during the October 16 robbery of the Tin Pan Resort in Nowata, Oklahoma. Several gold watches and rings were also found on the premises, including the stolen wedding ring belonging to the manager of the Metropolitan Hotel. The search also turned up a pair of silk gloves, which were traced to Centralia bank president T. R. Montgomery. A large collection of guns found hidden under a bed was identified as the property of the Isham Hardware store.

Shortly after the Coffeyville raid, Montgomery County officers raided the suspect's previous residence in nearby Independence, Kansas. The small house had been rented in the name of Mabel Brooks, one of the ladies captured in the Coffeyville raid. An assortment of stolen watches, jewelry, and guns were discovered hidden in the residence. Most of the plunder was later identified and claimed by the victims of the many recent outrages committed by the gang.

Authorities suspected the individual giving his name as Mack Roe, was in reality the notorious Oscar Poe. His lady companion, Mabel Brooks, vehemently swore she was his legal wife, although she claimed to have lost their marriage license. The other female suspect, later identified as Helen Weiman, claimed to be Will Hart's betrothed. The two women were kept under guard in a room located adjacent to the lobby of the city jail. An officer by the name of Thompson was sent to observe them. According to Thompson, at about ten P.M.. the evening of their arrest, a nervous Mabel Brooks abruptly stood up and hiked her dress over her hips before reaching into her corset pulling out a roll of bills that would choke a horse. She then thrust the wad at the shocked officer saying "Here, take this, I don't want it found on me, It belongs to the boys." The roll contained $1,190.

Meanwhile, in another part of the jail just outside the cell where Oscar Poe was being held, an angry T. R. Montgomery, the owner of the Centralia Bank, faced his one time tormenter. According to witnesses, when the pair first made eye contact, they launched into a mean spirited staring contest that lasted several minutes. Suddenly, the old man abruptly and without warning, pulled out a pistol pointing it at Poe's head saying, "Now, how do you like a gun pointed at your head?" Poe stared back unflinchingly at the banker, commenting "Be careful old man, I won't be locked up forever, and if I am, I have many friends outside this jail." Seeing the threat had no effect, the elderly Montgomery put his gun away and stomped out the door. Several officers standing nearby watched the scene in near shock; glad the old man had not shot the bandit in cold blood before their very eyes.

According to news reports, in the days following the bandit's apprehension, the arresting officers and private detectives were noted as being beside themselves with glee. It appears their good humor was motivated by the fact the insurance company representing the Centralia, Oklahoma, Bank had announced a reward in the amount of $2,000 would be paid out to the individuals who had participated in the pair's capture.

The following week, when Oklahoma authorities demanded the men's extradition, several difficulties arose. Firstly, the bandits refused to cooperate unless their women were released. Without their consent, a time-consuming extradition hearing involving the Kansas Governor was necessary. To add to this, County Attorney Ise with the support of the officers involved in the arrest, refused to turn over the bandits to Craig County, Oklahoma, authorities without written assurance of the reward being paid to the interested parties. Ignoring all this, Craig County Undersheriff Lee Mitchell and a deputy named Webb showed up in Coffeyville demanding the prisoners. The pair of lawmen was sent packing empty handed back to the "Sooner" state. Although witnesses from the two hotel robberies, Isham's Hardware, and the Nowata resort heist, had also identified the two men as the perpetrators in those crimes, lawmen didn't seem interested in pursuing that angle. They were obviously holding out for the reward money, which was only offered toward the duo's prosecution in the Oklahoma bank robbery case.

Meanwhile, the local papers were having a heyday reporting the special treatment the prisoners were receiving at the jail, where the pair was dining on porterhouse steaks, cooked to their specifications and delivered from a local café, as well as being provided fine cigars and good wine for their consumption. This state of affairs was further inflamed when Will Hart's brother, Harry, begin visiting the pair on a daily basis bearing gifts for the outlaws, seeming to come and go as he pleased. The situation turned into quite a scandal. Clearly some silver had crossed a few palms. When a local newspaper reported on the duo being issued new mattresses and feather pillows, an embarrassed City Judge Hanlon immediately had their luxuries taken away and demanded the prisoner's prompt removal to Oklahoma.

A few days after the bandit's arrest, Dr. Heuston, the owner of the boarding house where the pair had been apprehended, contacted police informing them a pair of rough looking men and a woman, showed up on his doorstep seeking the whereabouts of the missing boarders. In response, Patrolman Scott Thornton and City Marshal Ralph Fulton set up a surveillance post across the street. The following morning, a man was observed knocking on the landlord's door. The good doctor was not home, but his wife answered the door. The man, described as well dressed, demanded to know the present location of her ex-renters. Stalling, she feigned ignorance. About this time, the officers moved in. On seeing their approach, the caller asked Mrs. Heuston, "Who are those guys?" He then bolted into the house making a run towards the back entrance, where to his surprise another minion of the law had been stationed armed with a sawed-off shotgun. On being confronted by the patrolman and his oversized blunderbuss, the surprised suspect realizing the gig was up, immediately raised his hands in surrender. When searched, he was found in possession of over $1200 in cash and a large .45 caliber horse-pistol.

The suspicious visitor was handcuffed and hauled

down to the city jail where under intense questioning he gave his name as A. L. "Pony" Poe, a rancher from Okmulgee County. He claimed he was the Uncle of one of the apartment's ex-residents, Mack Roe. He further stated he had received a telegram the previous day from his nephew, asking him to come to his aid. On his arrival in Coffeyville, he immediately journeyed to his nephew's apartment where he found no one home, but decided to try again this morning. When questioned about the man and woman who had allegedly accompanied him on his first trip to the residence, he swore total ignorance of the event. He further claimed he had fled when approached by officers because he thought they were robbers. When lawmen inquired about the large sum of cash and gun found on his person when arrested, he stated he was a livestock buyer and had to carry large amounts of cash in his business and naturally needed protection in the form of a firearm. The man also denied any knowledge of his nephew's unlawful activities, but agreed to be escorted to Craig County, Oklahoma, for further questioning. The next morning, Oklahoma officers picked up their suspect and drove him to Vinita, the county seat, where he under went several days of intense grilling from authorities. He was then released

Boarding house row near Coffeyville, Kansas, circa 1920. Courtesy of the Kansas Historical Society

Old Craig County jail as it is today. Courtesy Naomi Morgan

for lack of evidence. According to news reports, the mysterious suspect had given officers a great deal of helpful information.

On November 7, after a deal was worked out guaranteeing Kansas lawmen their fair share of the reward and promising the bandits the release of their female companions, Craig County officers picked up Poe and Hart, transporting the pair to the Craig county jail in Vinita, Oklahoma. Both of the bandits' lady friends were released, but Montgomery County, Kansas authorities immediately re-arrested Mabel Brooks for possessing stolen goods in her home in Independence. Curiously, after being transported

Holding pen inside the old Craig County jail today. Courtesy Naomi Morgan

to the Vinita jailhouse the pair of suspected bandits refused to hire an attorney or seek legal assistance, a fact that baffled local authorities. Judge Ed Stanley appointed a local attorney, W. P. Thompson, to represent the pair at their preliminary hearing on December 1, where the defendants plead not guilty. A cash bond of $6,000 was set and the duo promptly bound over to the District Court for trial. Their trials (Craig county cases #1303 and #1304) were set to begin the following week.

On the day of the preliminary, Poe, who was still known as Mack Roe to authorities, was quoted as saying it was a waste of money for him to hire an attorney. Fearing the pair was planning a jailbreak, authorities decided to send the duo to the State prison to be kept for safekeeping until their trial.

At about 2 am December 5, the morning before the duo was to be transported to McAlester, Assistant Chief of Police Frank Smiley found a badly inebriated man collapsed near the Farmers State Bank in downtown Vinita. The officer hailed a taxi driven by Virgil Miller to transport the seemingly soused man to the "drunk tank" in the county jail to be held until he could sober up and face the local magistrate the following morning. On arrival at the jail, the miscreant seemed to suddenly sober up, requesting Officer Smiley and Jailor George Ellis to release him on bond. He pulled out a wad of cash asking if he could pay his fine, promising he would go straight home and sleep it off. While Smiley and the jailor were busy arguing over whether to agree to the drunk's request, the fellow, who turned out to be Russell Tucker, slipped over to the front door opening it. Suddenly, two armed men later identified as Lee Jarrett and Jess Littrell leapt into the room and overpowered the jailor forcing him to the floor. They then commenced to brutally beat the poor man with their

Exterior side entrance to the old Craig County jail today. Courtesy of Naomi Morgan

gun-butts and kick him in the groin and chest.

Upon getting hold of the jailor's keys and hand-cuffing both officers to a heavy table, the invaders dashed into the cell area releasing Poe and Hart. One of the outlaws, later identified as Littrell, asked if "any of you other jailbirds want to fly?" Luther Cox, a young man being held for auto-theft (Craig county court case #1294), answered "I'll go." He was let out of his cell to join the group. After locking the two officers into Poe and Hart's now empty cells, the escapees fled out the basement door still in possession of the jail's keys.

Marion Simerson, the day jailor, who lived in an apartment attached to the facility, heard the commotion. Suspecting the worst, he grabbed his .16 gauge shotgun loaded with birdshot and walked to the front of the building in time to see the group of outlaws escaping on foot. He took aim and fired both barrels at the

Interior stairway leading to the basement jail cells. Courtesy of Naomi Morgan

fleeing men. He later stated he was certain his shots had struck at least one of the individuals. The fugitives responded by firing several rounds his way. The jailor dived into an open doorway taking cover. A few moments later, J. L. Stephens, who lived nearby, saw six men run past his home on West Flint Street, getting into a large touring car. He stated he saw the barrels of their guns glistening in the moonlight.

Back at the jail, Marion Simerson grabbed the phone to call for help, but was greeted by a dead line. The outlaws had apparently cut the phone lines in several places around the town prior to their raid. Due to the loss of the jail's keys it took several hours of effort before the officers could be released from the cells the outlaws had locked them in. A large posse was organized and dispatched into every part of the county. There was no sign of the escapees and their cohorts. Incidentally, within days of the pair's escape, the Banker's Association retracted their offer to pay the Kansas officers the reward they had promised, implying since the men were no longer in custody, the reward was null and void. The Kansas lawmen reacted angrily, but their protests landed on deaf ears.

In the late afternoon of December 8, a new Ford car drove up to the front entrance of the State Bank in Alluwe, a small community eleven miles south west of Nowata. Three masked men alighted from the rig and leisurely strolled into the institution where Cashiers O. C. Chapman and Andy Calico were busy closing up for the day. Several customers stood in the lobby chatting with the bankers. Pistols were flashed and the witnesses were ordered to raise their hands over their heads. The trio of bandits, later identified as Oscar Poe, Will Hart, and Jess Littrell, gathered up the cash from the tills then rifled the vault for over $2,500. The witnesses were locked in the vault prior to the robbers casually walking out of the bank getting into the car driven by either Russell Tucker or Lee Jarrett. The automobile slowly drove out of town. A posse was quickly organized and sent in pursuit of the robbers, but to no avail.

Authorities suspected the getaway car used by the bandits was the same vehicle stolen from a rural Alluwe resident, Lon Scott, earlier that day. Lawmen stated they were certain the perpetrators were members of the recently dubbed Poe-Hart Gang. A $1,000 a head reward, dead or alive, was offered for the robbers by the Oklahoma Banker's Association.

Three days later, in the shadow of the Craig County Jail in nearby Vinita, two masked men dressed in dark suits and overcoats, entered the Farmers State Bank. At least one man, possibly two, sat in a large Ford touring car parked directly in front of the institution. Since it was the lunch hour, the bank's cashier, Jasper Martin, was alone in the building. He looked up observing the men enter the

Two views (front and side) of a safe found in a field near Stillwater, Oklahoma, that was blown with nitro around the turn of the century. The safe is on display at the Washington Irving Museum near Stillwater, Oklahoma. Courtesy Naomi Morgan

building and take up strategic positions in the main lobby. The lead bandit, suspected to have been Oscar Poe, stuck a large handgun in the frightened cashier's face declaring, "Give me the cash, and be damned handy with that currency, boy." Since the robber appeared to be deadly serious, the cashier immediately complied with his demands. Poe then escorted the banker to the vault where he and his partner, assumed to have been Will Hart, gathered up about $17,000 in cash and gold coin before locking the hapless cashier in the vault. On taking their leave, the bandits ripped

Advertisement for First State Bank of Alluwe, circa 1916.

The Way to Save

Deposit a few cents in your home bank each week—put it on Savings Deposit and let it draw interest. You are not only saving money—but you are being paid to do so. Open an account with our bank today. We solicit small accounts as well as large ones.

WE PAY FOUR PER CENT ON TIME AND SAVINGS ACCOUNTS.

DEPOSITS GUARANTEED

First State Bank of Alluwe
O. C. CHAPMAN, Cashier.

Farmers State Bank (right corner) circa 1918. Courtesy of Eastern Trails Museum

the banks telephone from the wall smashing it on the floor into a dozen pieces. Although the sidewalk and street in front of the bank was filled with pedestrians at the time of the robbery, it seems no one noticed anything out of the ordinary.

Walking back to the bank after a relaxing dinner in the café next door, Assistant Cashier Graham Paige was shocked to find a screaming Martin locked in the vault. Craig County Sheriff Lionberger and Vinita Chief of Police Bill Meeks were immediately notified of the robbery. A heavily armed posse was formed and sped in a half dozen cars west towards the Osage Hills where the gang was suspected to be heading. Vinita bank President John Wise, who had been a victim and witness to the Centralia bank robbery where he was personally robbed of his gold watch and $19 in cash, mused out loud that the motive of the bandits was revenge on him for testifying against the gang members in front of the Craig County Magistrate.

The Poe-Hart Gang was quickly turning out to be the most prolific bunch of thieves to hit the Oklahoma-Kansas border area since the Dalton Gang, who had been wiped out trying to rob two banks at once in Coffeyville, Kansas in 1892. The band, who had until recently, only targeted horses in their nefarious activities, had obviously found a more inviting target in the area's banks and businesses. Financial institutions in the area began hiring extra guards and lawmen in a four state area were put on high alert.

On the morning of December 20, citizens of the town of Skiatook, Oklahoma, which lies just north of the city of Tulsa, found the front door of the Oklahoma National Bank located in the heart of town, torn off it's hinges. When the town constable, followed by a group of curious citizens entered the institution to investigate, they found the bank's safe with its door blown off. It was apparent the contents of the box had been completely looted. Initially it was announced some $20,000 in cash and gold was missing. The number was later paired down to about $2,800 after a full accounting of the books had been made. Strangely, area residents had not heard the explosion in the bank, which had occurred sometime between midnight and 5 am. Osage County Sheriff Woolly told reporters that although there were few leads in the case, authorities did have a description given them by the station master at the railroad depot who had on the afternoon of the robbery, spotted two men attempting to cut the telegraph lines. One of the descriptions given by the station master perfectly matched that of one of the escapees from the Craig county jail, Oscar Poe, alias Mack Roe.

The following day, Oscar's Uncle Pony Poe, who had been inaccurately dubbed "Poem" Poe by the press, showed up at the Montgomery County courthouse in Independence, Kansas, with $750 in cash in an effort to bond out Mabel Brooks Poe, Oscar's common law wife. Shortly after releasing Mrs. Poe, officers studying the money Poe had given them, recognized some of the bills as coming from the Alluwe Bank, which had recently been robbed by her husband and Pony's nephew. Within a matter of days, lawmen from Nowata County traveled to the village of Nuyaka near Okmulgee and arrested Pony Poe for suspicion of complicity in the armed robbery of the Alluwe Bank. The old horse thief was quickly transported to the Nowata County by rail and lodged in the basement jail.

STATE OF OKLAHOMA,)
                    :ss.
COUNTY OF CRAIG,   )

IN THE Justice COURT.
of Ed. A. Stanley, Justice of
Peace in and for Vinita Township
Craig County ,Oklahoma.

STATE OF OKLAHOMA, - - - Plaintiff

VS.   No.   Criminal

Mack Roe and William Hart, Defendants

APPLICATION FOR ORDER TO PAY EXPENSES OF WITNESSES FROM WITHOUT THE COUNTY
OF CRAIG.

Comes now   Willard H. Voyles   County Attorney
of Craig County, Oklahoma, and represents to the Court that

E.W.Thompson, S.S.Thornton and Ralph Fulton have each

axdxbx   attended this court for the trial of the above entitled case as
witness   for the State in obedience to order of the Court, endorsed
upon the subpoena, directing the attendance of said witnesses which
order was signed by the Judge of this Court; said witnesses coming from
Montgomery   County, Kansas, pursuant thereto; That the said
witnesses and each of them so attending incurred expenses for railroad
fare, hotel bills, and lodging while in attendance this court for the trial
of the above entitled case, in the following sums, to-wit:

E.W.Thompson, Railroad fare, board ,lodging and other $10.00
S.S.Thornton   "   "   "   "   " $10.00
Ralph Fulton   "   "   "   "   " $10.00

WHEREFORE movant requests that an order be made authorizing and
directing the payment of said expenses to the said witnesses out of the
treasury of Craig County, Oklahoma, as provided by law in such case.

Craig County Court document of Roe (Poe) and Hart, robbery
charge.

STATE OF OKLAHOMA,)
) ss.   IN THE JUSTICE COURT.
COUNTY OF CRAIG,)   ED. A. STANLEY, JUSTICE OF PEACE
                           VINITA TWP. CRAIG COUNTY,
                               OKLAHOMA

STATE OF OKLAHOMA, - - - Plaintiff

       VS.   No.   Criminal

Mack Roe and William Hart   Defendants

ORDER FOR THE PAYMENT OF EXPENSES OF WITNESSES FOR THE STATE, FROM WITHOUT CRAIG COUNTY, OKLAHOMA.

          It having been made to appear to this Court that

                       Mark A. Shipley

has attended the trial of the above entitled cause in this Court, as a witness on behalf of the State, pursuant to a subpoena with an order endorsed thereon by this Court requiring his attendance, and that he is a resident of St.Louis, County, Missouri, and that he came in obedience to such subpoena from St. Louis, St.Louis County, Missouri, to attend said trial as such witness ; that in so doing he personally incurred expenses for railroad fare, transportation and board in the sum of $22.50 and that he is entitled to receive said expenses from Craig County, Oklahoma, under Section 6019 Revised Laws of 1910.

          IT IS THEREFORE ORDERED by the Court that said

    Mark A. Shipley   be paid the sum of $22.50   for said expenses out of the treasury of Craig County, Oklahoma, and the County Clerk of said Craig County, Oklahoma, is ordered to issue a warrant therefor, and the County Treasurer of said Craig County, Oklahoma, is directed to pay said warrant in said sum for the expenses of said witness.

          Dated at Vinita, Oklahoma, this the 1st day of December 1916.

                                           Judge of the   Justice   Court of
Vinita Twp.   Craig County, Oklahoma.

Court document of proceedings against Oscar Poe and William Hart.

Failure to make bail – William Hart – Craig County, 1916.

Subpoena of witnesses – Centralia Bank robbery case, Craig County.

Before ......Ed. A. Stanley.................................Justice of the Peace in and for

Vinita...Township, Craig County, Oklahoma.

STATE OF OKLAHOMA,   Plaintiff

VS.

William Hart   COMPLAINT.

Defendant

Before   Ed. A. Stanley ....Justice of the Peace within and for

Vinita ....Township, Craig County, Oklahoma;

personally appeared.................William T. Rye.......................................

on this, the ...30th...day of.........October.............1916..and says that on the...............

day of ......October.........., 1916., in the County of Craig and State of Oklahoma, one

William Hart

then and there being, did then and there, wilfully, unlawfully, knowingly, wrongfully and
feloniously make an assault in and upon T.R.Montgomery, T.C.Montgomery,
and Howard Montgomery, then and there officers in charge of the First
National Bank, a copporation, of Centralia, Oklahoma, with a certain
weapon, to wit: a pistol, then and there and thereby putting the said
T.R.Montgomery, T.C.Montgomery and Howard Montgomery in fear of immediate
injury to life and person, by then and there threatning to shoot the
said T.R.Montgomery, T.C.Montgomery and Howard Montgomery, and did then
and there by the use of said force and putting in fear, wilfully, unlawfully, wrongfully and feloniously and against the will of them, the said
T.R.Montgomery, T. C. Montgomery and Howard Montgomery, take, steal and
carry away from the possession of the said T.R.Montgomery, T.C.Montgomery
and Howard Montgomery and the First National Bank, a corporation, of
Centralia, Oklahoma, of which said Bank the said T.R.Montgomery, T.C.
Montgomery and Howard Montgomery were then and there officers in charge,
certain personal property, to wit: FIVE THOUSAND Dollars in good and
lawful money of the United States of America, not then and there the prope
of said William Hart, with the unlawful, wrongful and felonious intent
then and there on the part of him, the said William Hart, to rob and
deprive the said T.R.Montgomery, T.C.Montgomery, Howard Montgomery and
the First National Bank, a corporation, of Centralia, Oklahoma, of said
personal property and to convert the same to the use and benefit of
him the said William Hart,

contrary to the form of the Statutes in such cases made and provided against the peace and
dignity of the State.

*William Hart – armed robbery, statement of charges, Craig County,
Oklahoma.*

CRIMINAL WARRANT---- Justice of the Peace.

State of Oklahoma, County of Craig, ss.

To M.B.Lionberger, Sheriff, or any Constable of said Craig County:

Complaint upon oath, having been this day made before me, Ed. A.
Stanley, Justice of the Peace in and for Rxxx Vinita Township, said
County and State, by William T. Rye, alleging that the crime of Robbery
has been committed and accusing William Hart thereof, and alleging and
charging in substance that in Craig County, Oklahoma, on the ___ day of
October, 1916, one William Hart then and there being did then and there w
wilfully, unlawfully, knowingly, wrongfully and feloniously make an assault in and upon T.R.Montgomery, T.C.Montgomery and Howard Montgomery
then and there officers in charge of the the First National Bak, a
corporation, of Centralia, Oklahoma, with a certain weapon, to wit: a
pistol, then and there and thereby putting the said T.R.Montgomery,
T.C.Montgomery and Howard Montgomery in fear of immediate injury xtto
life and person by then and there threatning to shoot the said T.R.
Montgomery, T.C.Montgomery and Howard Montgomery and did then and there
by the use of said force and putting in fear, wilfully, unlawfully,
wrongfully and feloniously and against the will of them, the said T.R.
Montgomery T.C.Montgomery and Howard Montgomery, take, steal and carry
away from the possession of the said T.R.Montgomery, T.C.Montgomery,
and Howard Montgomery and the First National Bank, a corporation, of
Centralia, Oklahoma, ẟ which said bank the said T.R.Montgomery, T.C.
Montgomery and Howard Montgomery were then and there officers in charge,
certain personal property, to wit: FIVE THOUSAND Dollars in good and
lawful money of the United States of America, not then and there the
property of him, the said William Hart, with the unlawful, wrongful and
felonious intent then and there on the part of him the said William Hart,
to rob and deprive the said T.R.Montgomery, T.C.Montgomery and Howard
Montgomery and the First National Bank, a corporation, of Centralia,
Oklahoma, of said personal property and to convert the same to the use
and benefit of him, the said William Hart,

YOUR ARE THEREFORE C MMANDED FORTHWITH to arrest the above named
William Hart and bring him before me forthwith at my office in Vinita
Township, Craig County, Oklahoma, or in my absence or inability to act,
before the nearest and most accessible magistrate in this County.
WITNESS my hand this the 30th day of October, 1916.

Statement of charges against William Hart – Centralia Bank robbery, Craig County.

WARRANT

In the Justice Court of Nowata City Justice District, Nowata County,

State of Oklahoma. Before ALBERT PICKENS Justice of the Peace

THE STATE OF OKLAHOMA, Plaintiff

vs.

Jess Littrell, Oscar Poe, Billy Hart,   } Warrant of Arrest

Russell Tucker, Lee Jarrett, Albert
Conner and Pone Poe   Defendant. s

To the Sheriff or any Constable of Nowata County, Greeting.

Complaint upon oath having been made before me by C.F.Gowdy, County Attorney

that the offense of Robbery in the First Degree

has been committed and accusing Jess Littrell, Oscar Poe, Billy Hart, Russell
Tucker, Lee Jarrett, Albert Conner and Pone Poe ; You are therefore commanded to forthwith arrest
the above named Jess Littrell, Oscar Poe, Billy Hart, Russell Tucker,
Lee Jarrett, Albert Conner and Pone Poe
and bring him before me forthwith at my office.

Witness my hand this 3rd day of January, 191

Justice of the Peace.

Armed robbey charges – Poe-Hart Gang, Nowata County.

Chapter Four

Shootout at The "Big Blue"

At around three a.m. on January 6, 1917, an elderly man named Thornbrew was on his way to seek medical assistance for a sick family member. While driving past the downtown district of the small community of Delaware, six miles north of the county seat of Nowata, he noticed a carload of men parked on the roadside near the Garritson Meat Market. Thinking there was some sort of emergency he slowed and inquired if he could be of assistance. The men, who were armed with a variety of rifles and pistols menacingly approached Thornbrew's rig informing him they were government agents looking for booze peddlers. They also firmly advised the "Good Samaritan" to keep moving "as fast as his legs could carry him." Thornbrew, wisely deciding not to argue the point, did as he was instructed. As he proceeded toward his destination he noticed the back door of the nearby meat market was open and several people were milling about inside. Becoming alarmed of this activity, as well as the bizarre behavior of the so-called posse, he determined to contact authorities about his suspicions. When reaching the Doctor's residence he immediately picked up the phone and relayed his observations to thirty-one-year old Charles Bullock, the town Marshal.

On receipt of Thornbrew's information, Marshal Bullock in turn phoned John Garritson, who with his brother Ed were co-owners of the meat market, making arrangements to meet them at their store. On arrival at the business, Bullock and the Garretsons found a deserted scene.

The individuals Thornbrew had previously observed stand-ing about the area had departed. The trio also noticed the market's back door was standing open. The door's hinges had been pried off the frame. The Garritson brothers quickly took inventory of their stock and soon realized they were missing a recently dressed out whole hog and a host of other supplies.

The Marshal, now certain a crime had been commit-ted, began gathering a posse. On studying the tracks made by the suspect's car, Bullock noticed the tire treads left an unusual imprint. A car load of local vigilantes containing John and Ed Garritson, along with Lon Bingaman, presi-dent of the town council and Charles Barham, a local at-torney, began following the trail of the burglars. Shortly afterwards, another vehicle containing Marshal Bullock, a man named Harcleload, and Charlie Barham's teenage son Fred, sped out of town to catch up with the others. It was reported the posse members were armed with all man-ner of rifles and shotguns.

It appears shortly after the pursuit began the second car broke down. Bingham and Harcleload stayed with the disabled car while the other vehicle, now containing Mar-shal Bullock, the Barhams, and the Garritson brothers con-tinued with the chase. After more than ten hours on the

"Big Blue" country, prairie and bluffs. Courtesy of Naomi Morgan

road, the vigilantes had trailed the suspicious car tracks to a spot seven miles northeast of town on the edge of an area known as the Blue Canyon. The big gully, which was named for a blue haze, which sometimes settled over the abyss, was surrounded by thousands of acres of tall prairie grasses, which grew taller than a man's head. For decades the rugged, rock strewn, rattlesnake infested canyon with its caves and sinkholes had offered sanctuary for fugitives on the run. Throughout the Civil War period, members of Quantrell's Raiders sought refuge there from marauding union patrols. During the final decade of the nineteenth century the notorious Dalton brothers made use of the gorge while on the scout, carving their names on the steep canyon walls.

Located on the canyon's edge was the small colored community of Sanders. In Marshal Bullock's estimation, the thieves were probably residents of the isolated village. He had had trouble out this way before, pursuing and arresting several inhabitants of the little berg for the crimes of chicken theft and cattle rustling.

On arrival at the canyon's edge, a local black man named Bob Childers met the posse members. On questioning the individual, he stated the only strangers he had seen recently were some cowboys camped in the canyon who worked at the nearby Halsell ranch.

According to local lore, shortly after his meeting with the posse, Childers ran to the nearby Sanders schoolhouse, ringing a large bell in an effort to warn the outlaws of the officer's approach.

When the five-man posse began walking towards the lip of the nearby canyon they spotted a large Ford touring sedan parked on the edge of the incline, which matched the description given by Mr. Thornbrew in Delaware. Bullock apparently smelled a rat; he paused and informed the posse members they were up against something more than a hog thief. Thinking they might need re-enforcements, the posse began backing up towards their car, when suddenly young Fred Barham sighted movement to his side and yelled, "Look out." At that time, several men opened fire on the group from their rear and sides. Apparently, no one was hit in the initial volley, but a second barrage proved deadly. Marshal Bullock, struck by a single fatal bullet to the heart, pitched helplessly into the abyss. John Garritson, in an effort to find cover, began scrambling toward the canyon's edge. Suddenly, he toppled face first into the tall grass and lay motionless. Ed Garritson, close on his brother's heels, was hit once in the head and twice in the chest. He too fell into the gorge, his body-rolling end for end down the incline coming to rest on the valley floor. The Barhams dived into the tall grass and began scurrying towards the canyon's edge in an effort to find refuge as the ambushers fired a third volley which cut the tops off the tall weeds where the pair laid.

In the ensuing scramble to get out of the line of fire, young Fred Barham and his father became hopelessly separated. After crawling an estimated hundred yards down the canyon floor, the elder Barham discovered an adjacent gully, which connected into the main canyon. On crawling a few feet into the ravine Barham came upon a badly bleeding Ed Garritson propped up against a Blackjack tree.

Although the pair had walked and crawled a good distance from the original ambush site, they were not yet out of the woods. When the men emerged from the gully and attempted to cross an open field, their antagonists spotted them and opened fire with high-powered rifles on their exposed positions. The elder Barham's hat was shot off his head and a bullet nicked his lapel. The duo scrambled back into the cover of the ravine they had emerged from.

After traveling a few hundred yards further up the small gulch, the pair once more attempted a mad dash across the big meadow. For a second time the bad men hosed them down with a heavy barrage of gunfire. Barham, armed with a long-barreled pump shotgun reportedly returned fire. He stated he observed one of the attackers fall to the ground clutching his shoulder. At this point, the gunmen began a hasty retreat towards their car, stopping just long enough to set fire to the posses parked automobile.

Meanwhile young Barham, crawling in the opposite direction of where the fighting was taking place, rose up and began to run as fast as his young legs could carry him toward safety. He didn't stop until he hit Billy Barr's store seven miles away in Childers. On hearing the story told by the badly frightened and exhausted young man, Barr placed a phone call to the Nowata County Sheriff's office informing officers of the near massacre going on in the Blue Canyon. At about 4 P.M., Sheriff Gillespey gathered up a ten-man posse and once he made sure they were well armed and provisioned the group set off in a three-car caravan speeding toward the scene of the debacle. A call was also made to the Craig County Sheriff asking for re-enforcements. In response to their fellow officers request, Sheriff Lionberger, Deputy Webb, and Federal Marshal L. P. Smart, along with several armed volunteers, sped toward the scene of the ambush. On arrival at Childers, the Nowata posse questioned young Barham, who claimed the group of outlaws numbered fifteen to twenty individuals. The lad was brought along to guide the officers to the scene.

Back at the canyon Charlie Barham and his wounded companion laid low for more than an hour before they began walking down the ravine, finally emerging at the home of an elderly black woman near the little Sanders Post Office. Barham breathlessly pounded on the woman's door pleading with her to go for help. Feeling compassion for the pair of terrorized white men, she complied and immediately began journeying toward Childers, which was the location of the nearest telephone. While on the road, about halfway to her destination, the black woman met the posse led by Sheriff Gillespey. She delivered her message to the lawmen, who thanked her and set off in a cloud of dust toward Sanders in hope of saving the lives of the unlucky Garritson and the elder Barham.

When the posse arrived at Sanders, they located the unfortunate pair. The elder Barham was reportedly overwhelmed with happiness to find his young son still alive and well. Ed Garritson, suffering from wounds in the head, chest, and hip was speedily driven to the Nowata hospital for treatment. It was initially feared he would not survive his grievous wounds. Marshal Bullock's body was found lying about fifteen feet down the canyon's edge. John Garritson was found about thirty yards away lying in the tall grass. He was described as being in the throes of death, suffering from a severe head wound. Garritson was immediately transported to the Nowata Hospital to join his wounded brother.

Around this time, the posse from Vinita arrived. With a combined strength of some thirty men, the two groups began searching the deep crevices of the Blue. At the far end of the canyon, lawmen uncovered a cave with a large cache of foodstuffs, ammunition, and clothing. Some of the supplies were identified as stolen from the store at Coodys Bluff, which had been robbed by the gang immediately after the Centralia bank robbery. Hanging nearby was a whole hog. It was thought to be the one stolen from the Garritson store. Several straw beds and a stove were located nearby. The two black men found in the vicinity of the shootout, Bob Childers and Emmett Walden of nearby Sanders, were questioned. Walden admitted to bringing supplies to the gang and acting as their cook. Childers, who was found in possession of a pair of shoes, a knife, and a watch, which were identified as stolen from the Coodys Bluff store, admitted after some intense persuasion, the assassins from the canyon were Oscar Poe, Will Hart, Jess Littrell, Russell Tucker, and probably Lee Jarrett. After questioning all those involved, officers came to realize Fred Barham's story of fifteen to twenty gunmen was untrue.

Meanwhile, news of the ambush was relayed throughout the state via telephone, telegraph, and word of mouth. While the posse was looking over the canyon searching for clues, a carload of armed men were observed racing through nearby Nowata. An hour later, the same car was sighted in downtown Chelsea headed south. Rogers County authorities attempted to catch up with the suspicious rig, but met with no success. Adding to the confusion, information later came to light suggesting the gunmen may have sought refuge at the Jarrett farm, which was located just

Grave of John Garritson, killed at the "Big Blue" shootout. Courtesy Naomi Morgan

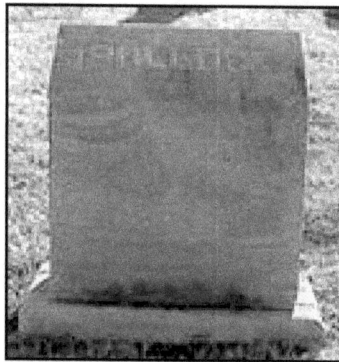

Grave of Officer Bullock, killed at the "Big Blue" shootout. Courtesy Naomi Morgan

east of Lenapah, in the immediate aftermath of the shootout.

At midnight, the posse gave up hope of capturing the assassins, returning to their respective homes. At about 1:30 am John Garritson died of his wounds. Residents of the little town of Delaware were stunned on receipt of the tragic news. Both Garritson and Bullock were very popular in the community. Ironically, both men were thirty-one-years old.

Marshal Bullock was buried at the Lenapah cemetery. Hundreds attended his funeral, including lawmen from all over the state. A local group sang the tune "Someday We'll Understand" in front of a misty eyed and still numb audience. His widow and two small children survived him. The day of his funeral, the city council of Delaware passed a resolution recognizing the sacrifice of their Marshal while engaged in protecting the lives and property of the citizens of the town. Every person of age in the little town signed the proclamation.

The following day, the remains of John Garritson was laid to rest about fifty feet from Officer Bullock's gravesite. His widow survived Garritson, who was one of Delaware's leading citizens. Nearly three hundred folks attended the funeral, which was officiated by a Reverend Summers of the Delaware Methodist church.

Map circa 1915 – Centralia area. Blue Canyon located just north of community of Sanders. Courtesy Muskogee Public Library.

STATE OF OKLAHOMA

vs.

Jess Littrell

Defendant.

In the _____ County _____ Court

of _____ Nowata _____ County, Oklahoma

IN THE NAME AND BY THE AUTHORITY OF THE STATE OF OKLAHOMA

Now comes _____ C. F. Gowdy _____ the duly qualified and acting County Attorney,

in and for _____ Nowata _____ County, State of Oklahoma, and gives the _____ County

Court of _____ Nowata _____ County, State of Oklahoma, to know and be informed that

_____ Jess Littrell _____

did, in _____ Nowata _____ County, and in the State of Oklahoma, on or about the _____ 6th

day of _____ January _____ in the year of our Lord One Thousand Nine Hundred and _____ Seventeen

and anterior to the presentment hereof, commit the crime of _____

_____ MURDER IN THE FIRST DEGREE _____

In the manner and form as follows, to-wit: That the said Jess Littrell acting in concert
and together with, Russell Tucker, Oscar Poe and Billy Hart, then and
there being, did then and there unlawfully, wilfully, feloniously, without
authority of law, with malice aforethought and with a premeditated design
to effect the death of one, John Garretson, did then and there make an
assault with a certain firearm, the exact nature of which is unknown, then
and there loaded with powder and leaden balls, and then and there had and
held in the hands of them, the said Jess Littrell, Russell Tucker, Oscar
Poe and Billy Hart and did then and there with the said firearm, the
exact nature of which is unknown, so had and held as aforesaid, unlawfully,
wilfully, feloniously and without authority of law, with malice aforethought
and with a premeditated design to effect the death of him, the said
John Garretson, fire, shoot and discharge the said firearm, the exact
nature of which is unknown at, against and into the body of him the said
John Garretson, and did then and there and thereby, without authority of
law, with malice aforethought and with a premeditated design to effect
the death of him the said John Garretson, inflict certain mortal wounds
in and on the body of him the said John Garretson, of which said mortal
wounds so inflicted as aforesaid the said John Garretson, did languish
and languishing, died on or about the 6th day of January, 1917, with the
unlawful, wilful and felonious intent in him, the said Jess Littrell to
murder and kill him the said John Garretson

contrary to the form of the statutes, in such cases made and provided, and against the peace and dignity of the State.

_____ County Attorney.

STATE OF OKLAHOMA
NOWATA COUNTY } ss

I, _____ C. F. Gowdy _____

being duly sworn, on oath state, that I have read the above and foregoing information and know the contents thereof and that
the facts stated therein are true.

_____

Jess Littrell – murder charge, Nowata County.

Chapter Five

The Manhunt

On the morning of January 11, a trio of young ladies approached Okmulgee Deputy Sheriff John Lung reporting the suspicious behavior of three men they had made the acquaintance of the previous night at a dance hall resort near the Okmulgee County mining town of Henryetta. The men, whom the women described as spending money like drunken sailors in port, had introduced themselves as horse buyers from Craig County, Oklahoma. The ladies were apparently quite taken with the swashbuckling characters, spending the bulk of the evening dancing and flirting with them. As the night wore on, one of the individuals, who had been nipping on a well-concealed pint of whiskey, began bragging he and his companions were responsible for the recent Skiatook bank robbery. He further stated the trio aimed to hold up the Bank of Okemah in the next few days.

After viewing a stack of mug shots, the ladies identified two of the Romeos as Russell Tucker and Jess Littrell. An immediate alarm was issued notifying all area officers to be on the lookout for the pair. Okmulgee County Sheriff Claude Roach ordered armed sentries posted at the banks at Henryetta and Okmulgee. When notified of the threat to the Okemah bank, which was in Okfuskee County, Sheriff Barry Jones also stationed several deputized guards at that institution.

On Friday afternoon, January 12, a Ford touring sedan parked in front of the First National Bank of Harrah,

Oklahoma, a community of 500 souls located twenty-six miles east of Oklahoma City. An individual recognized as Russell Tucker, stayed at the wheel of the vehicle keeping the motor running while three unmasked men bailed out of the rig and began making their way towards the bank's front entrance. One of the bandits, identified as Jess Littrell took up a station at the main door while Oscar Poe along with Will Hart entered the building. Present in the institution at the time were Bank President B. F. Miles and Clerk A. G. McClurg who were going about their assigned duties. Oscar Poe armed with a long barreled Colt pistol ordered the bankers to "reach for the sky." The employees were then forced at gunpoint to lie on the floor while the pair rifled the cash drawers and safe. As the robbers were leaving, Poe noticed a diamond stickpin attached to McClurg's tie. He reached down and cut the tie off with his pocketknife, attaching the stickpin to his own vest. Both bankers were herded into the vault and locked in. The bandits then bounded down the bank's steps loading into the parked Ford. Their fleeing automobile was observed by witnesses traveling east out of town at a high rate of speed.

A few minutes after the bandits fled the institution, the pair of bankers liberated themselves with a handy screwdriver and gave the alarm. A posse, made up of five carloads of armed residents, was quickly assembled and began a pursuit of the outlaws. Within the hour other large groups of heavily armed men from the nearby towns of Meeker, Prague, Paden, and Boley organized and began setting up roadblocks at bridges and crossroads throughout the area. That night, an Okfuskee County posse found the bandit's getaway car abandoned on the roadside near Paden, Oklahoma, five miles northeast of Prague. Apparently, the fugitives had discarded the vehicle after it suffered a blown tire. Loose change and a box of cartridges, along with several items of clothing were recovered from the rig.

The following day, officers arrested three local men, charging them with looting the bank. Although authorities seemed certain they had nabbed the guilty party, the trio was quickly cleared of the crime. It was later ascertained the bank's losses totaled nearly $4000 in cash and gold coins.

There was no news of the robber band until four days later when Harrah Bank President B. F. Miles spotted Jess Littrell and another man who turned out to be Russell Tucker, at the Rock Island depot dismounting an incoming passenger train. The inquisitive banker followed the pair to the doorstep of the home of Joe Welsher, located two miles southeast of town, before notifying the local police. Why two of the bandits returned to the scene of the crime after they had apparently made a clean getaway is unknown. Meanwhile, a large posse organized by Sheriff G. E. Johnson of Oklahoma County, quickly traveled to the Welsher home surrounding the residence. A posse man, Pearl Carpenter, brother-in-law to Joe Welsher, was sent into the house to talk the fugitives into abandoning their resistance or at least releasing Welsher's wife and children, who were being held hostage. Negotiations dragged on for several hours before Carpenter walked out of the residence at 3 am stating the fugitives had agreed to give up.

According to statements made later that day by Sheriff Johnson in an interview with reporters, the posse had high expectations at that point for a peaceful conclusion to the siege. After waiting about fifteen minutes for the outlaws to appear, the pair of brigands, surrounded by Welsher's wife and children, suddenly burst out of the home's back door and began running across a cornfield toward a nearby wood line. The posse, taken aback by this unexpected development, held their fire fearing they would hit the innocent hostages who were being used as human shields. The pair of outlaws, having no such misgivings, fired several volleys towards the lawmen wounding Deputy Sheriff Joe Layton in the leg and grazing another posse man.

Posse member Frank Carter, who was also the Sergeant-Of-Arms for the Oklahoma State Legislature in nearby Oklahoma City told reporters when interviewed, "Pearlie came out of the house stating the desperadoes had agreed to give up, but all of a sudden the pair came bursting out the back door running towards the woods pushing the woman and kids in front of 'em. One fella shot the cowboy hat off my head; I took deliberate aim at the man, firing three shots. I thought I hit him, but not one of the shots took effect. I think they were wearing body armor." He further stated, "I believe in the future, I'll stick to my office job."

Another posse man identified as James Beaty, the County Clerk, told newsmen, "When the shooting started, I ran towards the house, but got hung up in a barbed wire fence. During the gunfight, I could neither advance nor retreat. I felt the breeze as the bandit's bullets passed by my head." he further elaborated, he would, "never be so foolish as to join another posse."

Shortly after the fugitives made their way into a wooded ravine, they released their hostages and skeddaled towards the nearby North Canadian River bottoms. A brief manhunt ensued, but it didn't seem the posse had their hearts in it. After conducting a brief interrogation, Joe Welsher was arrested and charged with harboring the felons. Authorities misidentified the fugitives at the time as Walter Williams and Joe Buckner. Both names turned out to be aliases used by Tucker and Littrell.

Within minutes of the Harrah shootout telephone and telegraph wires began humming, issuing lookout warnings to every Sheriff's office and police department in a six county area. Huge posses of armed vigilantes were organized, setting up roadblocks and swarming over the countryside in search of the fugitives. One reason for the enthusiastic participation of so many determined citizens was the fact the Oklahoma Banker's Association was offering a $5,000 cash reward for the bandits, dead or alive.

Shortly after dawn, three carloads of officers bumped into the fugitives just south of Harrah, driving a freshly stolen Dodge touring car. After a brief but intense fire fight, the posse, taken aback by the fugitive's fierce show of resistance, suddenly backed off allowing the outlaws room to escape. At noon, another posse cornered the desperadoes in a barn near Newalla. Again, there was a sharp exchange of gunfire between the two parties. The motley group of vigilantes, made up of a dozen hastily recruited farmers and teenage boys equipped with a variety of worn out single barrel shotguns and .22 caliber rifles were no match for the well armed pair of brigands who possessed large caliber modern repeating rifles. Feeling the reception was a bit too hot for their liking, the posse once again gave ground permitting the pair time to escape, only this time afoot. The car they had stolen was recovered. When the rig was searched by lawmen, they found several discarded pieces of clothing, blood stains on the seats, and a half empty pint of homemade "wildcat" whiskey. Later that afternoon, the fugitives were spotted on foot near the tiny Lincoln County settlement of Midway. Several posses rushed to the area but drew a blank.

At around ten P.M.. a dead tired D. M. Fuller, who operated a part time taxi service in Meeker, took his shoes off and reclined in bed after a long day of chasing the out-laws with a posse made up of his Lincoln County neigh-bors. He and his fellow man-hunters had been beating the bush ever since the local town constable received news of the gunfight in Harrah. They had no luck in their endeavor and disbanded about 9 P.M., tired and discouraged. He had just dozed off when he was suddenly awakened by a loud rap on the door. On answering the knock, he observed two men, who he described as roughly dressed and dirty. The pair inquired if he would drive them to nearby Prague for $15 cash money. Although Fuller was tired and nearly played out, he answered in the affirmative. He needed the dough. Upon reaching their destination, the pair demanded to be driven to Boley, fifteen miles distant. They offered him an additional ten dollars for his services. By this time, the taxi man had become suspicious of the pair, figuring they could very well be the fugitives he and his friends had chased through the brambles earlier that day. When

getting gas at a fill-ing station he whis-pered to the atten-dant, that he was be-ing forced to drive the men, who he now suspected to be the outlaws, to the nearby black com-munity of Boley.

Sheriff Berry Jones and unidentified child circa 1917. Courtesy of Okfuskee County Historical Society

Fuller told the clerk to contact the law and explain his predicament. After filling his rig with petrol, Fuller and his cargo of desperadoes motored into the night towards Boley.

About 3 a.m., Okfuskee County Sheriff Barry Jones received a call informing him of poor Mr. Fuller's dilemma. Jones immediately set about organizing a posse. When the officers arrived in Boley at dawn, the fugitives were still in town trying to line up another car in order to continue their journey. The lawmen immediately began conducting a house-to-house search for the bandits. The bad men, somehow becoming aware of the officers presence, fled the scene by hijacking a colored schoolteacher named Floyd, who was traveling in a one-horse buggy towards the IXL School, where he was employed. On reaching a point three and a half miles northeast of Boley, the fugitives bailed off the rig setting their captive free. Continuing on foot, the bandits made their way to the nearby residence of a black tenant farmer named Robert Williams and began pounding on his door. When the unsuspecting sharecropper greeted the pair, the fugitives inquired if they could buy a spread of biscuits and gravy and hire him to transport them in his buckboard to the nearby village of Welty. They offered to pay him ten dollars, adding they would not take no for an answer.

Meanwhile, back in Boley, a citizen approached Sheriff Jones claiming to have seen two suspicious men riding in a buggy with a "nigra" teacher who taught at the IXL School. He further stated, when he saw it last, the buggy was traveling "lickety-split" towards the tiny IXL community. He had also observed a passenger in the buggy having something in his hand poking it firmly into the ribs of his host. Sheriff Jones sent two carloads of men speeding in hot pursuit. The lead car contained Undersheriff W.

O. Green, the ex-Warden of Oklahoma's Granite Prison, along with Deputies Lafayette M. Boulware, Rice McKennon, and a colored officer named John Owens. Occupants of the second rig were Paden Town Marshal Lee Coleman, in addition to Officers P. W. Dewebar, Guy Harrison, and Chester Chambers of Boley. Sheriff Jones and Constable Allen Cash stayed in town investigating another lead before following their fellow officers.

Just moments after the arrival of the posse members at the schoolhouse, they observed the teacher's buggy traveling towards their location at a furious gait. When the overwrought educator informed officers he had just left the fugitives at the Williams's home a mile and a half west of their present location, the collection of officers commanded by Undersheriff Green hopped in their rig speeding off in that direction. Marshal Coleman's group was delayed a few minutes due to a mechanical problem with their vehicle.

When the group of officers arrived at Williams's home, they fanned out encircling the residence. When Deputy Green knocked on the front door, a nervous black man greeted him. When asked by the lawman if he had seen any white men in the area, he at first denied it, then abruptly fled from the home screaming they were inside eating. Suddenly, the pair of outlaws bolted out the back door running toward a nearby cotton patch with the quartet of officers hot on their heels. Tucker sped into the field while Littrell wisely sought cover in a nearby chicken house According to a statement made by John Owens, both outlaws fired on the officers while taking flight. Owens, Boulware, and Green returned fire striking Tucker several times. The outlaw dropped to the ground a total of three times on his run for freedom before finally "hitting the dirt with a loud thud and staying put," after being shot in the head by Deputy Boulware. By this time, the second group of officers had arrived and joined in the fray. Witnesses state after Tucker's death there was a pause in the action while lawmen, who had taken cover in and around a rock barn, inquired if Littrell wanted to surrender. Littrell, hiding behind the chicken house armed with a Savage 32-40 caliber rifle, answered them with a cascade of bullets, several which struck Deputy Boulware and another knocking Owens's hat off his head. In response to seeing his cap go flying, the black officer wisely hit the dirt, crawling to cover. He and several others in the posse then heard Littrell taunt Boulware, who was lying in the dirt, badly wounded, calling for him to "Get up and come get me you son of a bitch", to which the suffering deputy responded "I can't, you've shot me to death". The dying lawman was also overheard to say, " I wish I hadn't came here." At this point, the brave deputy let out a long audible moan and lay motionless.

In response to Boulware's death, the posse began blasting the chicken house with all manner of firearms, nearly shredding the building. Littrell soon cried "Uncle" screaming to the lawmen he desired to give up. The posse held their fire while the bandit, who had by this time been

Grave of Russell Tucker. Courtesy Naomi Morgan

Grave of Deputy L. M. Boulware. Courtesy R. D. Morgan

wounded five times, laid down his arms and came stumbling out from cover, his face and chest covered in blood and hands held high in the air. According to officers, nearly a hundred rounds had been exchanged between the two parties in the gun battle, which lasted an estimated fifteen minutes.

On searching the dead and wounded bandits, about $1,400 in cash was recovered along with Harrah Banker A. G. McClurg's expensive diamond stickpin, which was returned to the gentleman. Undertaker N. L. Eaton removed Boulware's body to his home in nearby Castle, where it was ascertained the deputy had suffered a total of three wounds, two which had passed through his upper torso and a third to the leg, striking an artery. The undertaker surmised it was this last injury, which had apparently

Street scene, circa 1917, Okemah, Oklahoma. Courtesy of Okfuskee County Historical Society.

caused the lawman's death, which he attributed to blood loss. Russell Tucker's bullet riddled corpse was removed to Eaton's undertaking parlors in Okemah, the county seat. Officers stated the outlaw's finger had to be pried off the trigger of his Winchester rifle. Undertaker Eaton later testified Tucker had seven separate bullet holes in his body, but it was obvious the wound to his forehead had caused his immediate demise.

The following morning, hundreds of citizens lined up to view Tucker's remains, which were propped up in the basement of Eaton's combination funeral home and hardware store. The morbidly curious sightseers plodded

Deputy Boulware's widow (second wife) and children, circa 1917. Courtesy Joe Tucker.

past the grisly sight for two days before Tucker's wife, by way of her attorney, John Ezzard of Claremore, claimed the body, having it prepared, then shipped by rail to his hometown of Nowata. Tucker's funeral was held at his sister's residence, where a crowd of several hundred curiosity seekers thronged the house and street from the time the body arrived until it's removal for interment at the Nowata Cemetery later that afternoon.

The following day's issue of the Claremore News reported the fact that Tucker's wife, Bertha, was currently a resident of Claremore, where she worked as a waitress, sharing a small apartment in the downtown district with her mother. The story went on to state, the widow was expected through her attorney to make a claim for the cash found on her slain husband's person and the car abandoned by the fugitives near Prague. It appears the title to the automobile had Tucker's name on it.

Deputy Lafayette "Fate" Boulware was laid to rest

Railroad Depot, circa 1918, Okemah, Oklahoma. Courtesy Okfuskee County Historical Society.

several days later at the Castle cemetery. The Missouri born lawman had settled in Castle around the turn of the century. The popular officer had been a lawman in the area since 1902. Boulware, who was known as a tough and fearless officer also had a reputation as a bit of a shootist, having shot and killed a man named Mike Kirk, in the line of duty in the summer of 1909.

Jess Littrell was arrested and taken to the Okemah jail by Sheriff Jones. After holding him there for a few hours, the lawman decided it was too dangerous to keep the badly wounded assassin in town. The mood of the city was ugly. Deputy Boulware had been a very popular officer blessed by a host of friends. Talk of a lynching was growing by the hour. Jones, fearing vigilantes might storm the jail in order to conduct a necktie party, decided to move his prisoner out of harm's way by transporting the outlaw to the state prison in McAlester by rail. Around midnight, under the cover of darkness, Jones had the gravely wounded bandit carried on a stretcher to the railroad depot where he and six heavily armed officers, along with a nurse, boarded the regularly scheduled southbound passenger train. The group made it as far as Holdenville where they stopped for the night and summoned a physician, when Littrell took a turn for the worst. After examining the bandit, the doctor's prognosis was grim. He expected the outlaw to expire by morning due to the damage caused by a bullet wound to his right lung. According to witnesses on the scene, Sheriff Jones fell into a state of extreme annoyance on hearing the news, fearing the killer would die prematurely, thus "Cheating the Hangman." Littrell proved to be a tough and resilient character, after a few days rest his condition improved to the point the group was able to continue their journey to the state pen. On arrival, he was lodged in the prison hospital under heavy guard. Incidentally, when correction officers searched his person they discovered a roll of cash amounting to $180 and a small dagger sewn into the outlaws long handled underwear.

Chapter Six

Ambush at Nuyaka

With the slaying of Russell Tucker and the capture of Jess Littrell, area lawmen were now able to concentrate their efforts in an all out push to kill or capture the remaining gang members who had escaped detection in the aftermath of the Harrah robbery. A break in the case came only a few hours after the Boley shootout when Okmulgee County Sheriff Claude Roach received a tip by telegraph concerning the possible whereabouts of the missing fugitives. The message, which originated from Nowata County, stated authorities there had garnered information from a confidential source pinpointing the sites of two of the gang's hideouts in rural Okmulgee County. The wire further stated, three officers, Nowata Deputy Sheriff Buck George, along with Chelsea policeman, Hiram Stevens, and a Burns Detective operative named Gustavason, would be arriving in Okmulgee the evening of the 18th. The communication went on to request assistance from local lawmen in planning a raid on the fugitive's hidden lair.

With over $1,000 (dead or alive) cash reward being offered for each of the outlaw's apprehension it's a good bet Sheriff Roach and his deputies were thrilled at the prospect of assisting the out of town man-hunters in their quest. In fact, numerous Okmulgee lawmen and vigilantes had been manning roadblocks and sweeping the area roads and woods for over a week in hopes of capturing the slippery fugitives.

Although the name of the subject who supplied the confidential information to Nowata officers has never been made public, there seems to be three likely sources. First is Luther Cox, the seventeen-year-old youth who escaped from the Vinita jail with Poe and Hart. After spending a few weeks with the bandit band, the spirited teen abandoned his fellow fugitives seeking refuge at the home of his parents in Sapulpa, Oklahoma. On informing his father of his adventures of the past month, he was advised to turn himself in and clear his conscience. On surrendering to authorities he was transported back to Craig County where lawmen were overjoyed to make accommodations for the lad in the county's "Cross Bar Hotel."

According to news reports, when Cox was formally questioned, he launched into a rambling highly fictional discourse of his adventures which consisted of not only protesting his own innocence of any criminal activity, but his adamant refusal to implicate his companions in any acts of wrong-doing. He did admit his traveling buddies had been Poe, the Harts, Littrell, Tucker, and Jarrett, although he vigorously attempted to alibi them on the dates of the robberies and murders which authorities were certain they had been involved. The lad also stated Oscar Poe claimed his next venture would include the robbery of three banks at once, thus beating the records of both the James and Dalton Gangs who had attempted but failed in their efforts to stick up two banks at the same time. Furthermore, Cox declared Poe intended on fleeing to Mexico as soon as he made a big haul.

After several days of intense grilling, young Cox was hauled before a magistrate where he plead guilty to a charge of car theft, the original crime he was being held on prior to his escape. The jurist took into consideration his limited cooperation with police and gave the boy a break, sentencing him to a mere two years in Oklahoma's Granite Reformatory.

The second and third suspected informants were the wounded and jailed Jess Littrell and Pony Poe, who was still a guest of the taxpayers at the Nowata County Jail. The theories concerning this pair will be further expanded on as the story progresses.

The trio of lawmen from up north arrived in Okmulgee around 1 a.m. on the morning of January 19. Sheriff Roach and Okmulgee Chief of Police Mel Bowman promptly joined them, along with two of Roach's deputies, William Robbins and John Lung. The latter two officers were a welcome addition to the posse, both being noted man hunters and legendary shootists.

Deputy "Wild Bill" Robbins, as he was known to his fellow lawmen, was an ex-Muskogee County deputy and Federal Marshal who was born in Arkansas and immigrated to the Indian Territory in 1892. He started his career in law enforcement on horseback serving as a deputy for "Hanging" Judge Isaac Parker, working out of Fort Smith, Arkansas with the likes of Marshals Paden Tolbert and Heck Thomas. Robbins had reputedly been involved in nearly a dozen gunfights in his storied career. He had only recently come to work for the Okmulgee County Sheriff's Department. According to newspaper reports, the deputy carried with him on the upcoming raid a Winchester 44-40 rifle he had recently purchased in Muskogee from the legendary ex-US Marshal Bud Ledbetter.

By far, the most colorful and controversial member of the posse was, John O. Lung. The future deputy was born in Arkansas in 1882. When Lung was still in his early teens, his family immigrated to the Oklahoma Territory where they established a small ranching operation. Legend has it; he learned to use a gun at an early age, quickly becoming a crack shot with all manner of firearms. In 1910, he was hired as a patrolman for the Oklahoma City Police

Department. Lung served with distinction until one night in 1913 when he became involved in an argument with the city's Chief of Police W .B. Nichols. He must have taken the argument personally because the following day when the two met, Lung, who was described as being in an state of extreme drunkenness, shot the Chief three times, once in the hand and twice in the left leg. One of the missiles passed through the chief striking Assistant Jailor J. R. Bittle, who was standing in the adjoining office, in the hip. Although he was originally charged with attempted murder, the charges were later dropped. His only punishment for the shooting fray seems to have been his prompt dismissal from the force.

In 1915, Okmulgee's Mayor M. F. Moroney recruited the out of work lawman to serve as an officer there. In the past two years, the town had experienced an oil and gas boom. Predictably, coming hand in hand with the sudden economic expansion was an influx of pickpockets, thieves, prostitutes, bootleggers, and other parasitic lowlifes hard on the trail of a fast buck. These unscrupulous individuals made separating the oil field workers from their hard earned cash an art form.

Although Lung, like many lawmen of the era, had a reputation of being a bit overzealous and brutal in carrying out the duties of his office, he was exactly the type of officer the Mayor had in mind for the job. Ironically, these same traits, which folks today would frown upon, made him a welcome sight to businessmen and honest citizens of the town.

Officer John Lung.
Photo courtesy of the
Okmulgee Daily Times

He was by all accounts a tough character. The local newspaper reported that although the town elders appreciated his ability to knock heads together, the deputy did have one major flaw in his character. As was witnessed at his previous place of employment where he had assaulted his fellow officers, the lawman occasionally had a habit of getting intoxicated and going on unpredictable and violent benders. Okmulgee residents often witnessed the grossly inebriated lawman in the act of motoring up and down the main street of town shooting out windows and challenging all comers to a duel. Lung, who ran for county sheriff three times, was according to news reports of the day, defeated at the polls due to his odd behavioral problems. The mayor put up with his nonsense for several years before requesting him to step down from his position. His unemployment lasted but a short time due to newly elected county Sheriff Claude Roach being in need of a deputy with his particular talents. Within days of his hiring, Lung was assigned to capture an escapee from the County Jail. The Deputy reportedly tracked the fugitive all the way to

The Deep Fork River near the Nuyaka Mission.
Courtesy Naomi Morgan

California where he shot and killed the man in a gun duel when he resisted arrest. In the next 24 hours, if all went according to plan, the brash lawman's expertise as a pistelero would soon be put to the test.

Armed with their information and all manner of the deadly and modern firearms, the Okmulgee posse was joined just north of town by the trio of officers from the north. The party of grim faced lawmen drove slowly toward the Nuyaka Mission on treacherously slick icy roads in a three-car caravan. It was bitterly cold with an inch of snow covering the ground when they arrived at nearly 4 a.m., at the Mission, which in reality was a Creek Indian Boarding School, located just east of Pony Poe's ranch. From information received from their sources, the lawmen knew the bandits had two hideouts in the area. The first was located about three miles west of the old Mission on the far side of the Deep Fork Canadian River. The area, known today as McDaniel's Bend, was and still is an incredibly rugged and isolated region. The cave the outlaws

Modern day view of spring where Nuyaka shootout occurred.
Courtesy of R. D. Morgan

had made their headquarters was situated in a deep, nearly inaccessible chasm known as "Hell Hole" Canyon. The area, serviced only by a narrow, rock-strewn path was virtually impossible to approach with out being seen. The second hideout was located three and one half miles northeast of the canyon on the east side of the river, next to a large spring, just north of Pony Poe's cabin. A rough cattle trail snaked across the adjacent pasture making it's way from Poe's ranch to the wooded spring.

After conferring with Deputy Lung, who had hunted deer near the gang's canyon hide out the previous winter, Sheriff Roach chose to attempt to ambush the bad men at the more assessable spring camp. From the Mission, the posse slowly made their way on foot trudging a half mile down the trail across a field and into a heavily timbered area which housed the site of the bandit's encampment next to the spring. On approaching the fugitive's lair, the disappointed posse discovered only a deserted campsite containing an empty tent and a cold fire ring. In statements made later that afternoon to the press by Deputy Robbins and Detective Gustavason, the posse decided to make the best of the situation by taking up positions around the camp hoping the fugitives would eventually show up at the spot.

Bowman, acting as the party's lookout, took the lead position stationing his self in front of the group at a point where the trail entered the thicket, which enclosed the spring. Lung, Robbins, and Stevens, armed with high-powered rifles, hid behind a nearby embankment, while Sheriff Roach, Gustafson, and Buck George, all armed with shotguns and pistols, took cover behind a series of tree stumps and large rocks behind them.

A brisk frigid wind kicked up causing the men to shiver on the moonless night. After a freezing three-hour wait, the sun finally began creeping up over the nearby praire; it's rays providing a small amount of warmth to the bone chilled lawmen. Around half past eight, Bowman stepped on to the cow path to answer the call of nature. While taking care of his business, he heard a faint noise further up the trail, near the far edge of the clearing. After a wait of a few minutes which seemed to him like hours,

January 19, 1917, headlines in the Tulsa Democrat. Courtesy of the Tulsa Democrat

he was able to make out a group of men about fifty yards away, entering the snow swept field plodding toward his position. Suddenly, one of the men, later known to be Harry Hart, sensing Bowman's presence, hollered "posse." Hart then fired two rounds from his rifle at the lawman. One bullet went wild, but the other clipped a tree limb next to Bowman's position. Flying bark and wood splinters struck the officer in the hand causing a ragged flesh wound.

Seconds after Hart opened up with his rifle, Poe and Will Hart joined in the fray running toward Bowman's position, spraying the far edge of the clearing indiscriminately with their Winchesters. Around this time, all seven members of the hidden-posse opened fire on the outlaw's positions. Harry Hart was quickly put out of commission by a well-aimed head shot delivered by the injured Bowman, striking the fugitive in the area of his left eye. The bandit crumpled in a heap by the side of the trail.

At least two of the many missiles directed at Oscar Poe struck the bandit in the upper torso. He stumbled, but quickly raised himself to an upright position, firing his rifle until empty. The badly wounded but determined outlaw then pulled a Colt six-shooter from under his coat and continued blazing away in the direction of the posse. After being struck several more times, Poe again fell to the ground and started crawling off the trail seeking cover, still firing his pistol. Will Hart, struck in the chest, arm, and head, tumbled headlong into the snow where he lay motionless. The posse, seeing they were getting the better of the bad men charged the downed trio firing their weapons as fast as they could. According to Robbins, Oscar Poe, whose face he could plainly see, was bleeding profusely from a wound to his jaw and crawling on all fours. In a final act of defiance, the tough outlaw turned toward the deputy firing a round from his pistol, the bullet striking the ground at the lawman's feet. Robbins returned fire with his Winchester 44-40, the projectile striking Poe in the forehead, killing him instantly.

By the time the charging posse men reached the fallen trio, it was evident they were all dead or dying. John Lung stated he heard Oscar Poe take one last gasp of air then be still. Five minutes and 100 rounds after it had began, the ambush abruptly ended. Except for the flesh wound to Chief Bowman's arm, the posse had dealt a deadly blow to the remnants of the gang and came out unscathed.

On searching the gunmen's bodies, Sheriff Roach reportedly found only $200 in cash and coin. This was an interesting development, considering the gang had stolen an estimated $50,000 in cash and gold coin in their short careers. Since only $3,500 had been found on Tucker and Littrell the previous day at Boley, this left a lot of unaccounted cash floating around. The mystery of the missing money has never been solved. There are many theories about what happened to the loot. One rumor, which surfaced in the days following the ambush, implied the posse members absconded with the booty. Another legend has the dead bandits hiding their ill-gotten gains in the small cave near their McDaniel Canyon hideout. Numerous Nuyaka residents have unsuccessfully searched the area repeatedly over the past 80 years looking for the lost plunder. *(At this point, I'll add a note of caution to any reader who is inclined to be a treasure hunter.) The area of the Deep Fork Canyon, where it is likely the bandits hid their treasure, if they hid any at all, is an extremely rugged, snake infested district. An explorer there is greeted by everything from sheer drop-offs to hidden sinkholes, which riddle the area. One can easily be turned around and become hopelessly lost in these canyon lands.

Another tale, which has been floating around the past

eight decades, refers to the manner the suspects were shot. A lot of folks wondered aloud how all three men received fatal head shots. Since shooting a moving man in the head at forty to fifty yards can be a difficult thing to accomplish, it has long been suspected the posse had simply crept up on the bad men and shot them in their sleep. It would be hard to blame the officers if this theory was true. As noted earlier in the story, the gang had already taken the lives of three lawmen and wounded several others. Although it would have obviously been an act of assassination, pure and simple, it must be remembered, the men were wanted, dead or alive. A final supposition put forth implies one or more of the posse men inflicted a coup-de-gras on the wounded bandits as an insurance policy they would cease resistance. Since all seven-posse men, who were the only living witnesses to the ambush, agreed with the description of the events given in the preceding pages, their version is the only one we have to go on.

After the ambush, the bodies of twenty-seven-year-old Oscar Poe and twenty-two-year-old Will and Harry Hart were laid out under a willow tree near the spring while officers searched the area looking for the missing loot. Presently, a passel of schoolchildren from the nearby Nuyaka Mission ambled across the pasture that separated the Mission and the spring, curious to see what all the excitement was about. According to researcher Bill Spears who has written a history of early day Nuyaka, several of those students continued to tell the story of seeing the bandits laid out on the ground "stone dead," for decades to come.

Around the noon hour, the officers wrapped the outlaw's bodies in sheets made from their tent loading them into the three cars for the slippery drive back to Okmulgee. On arrival in town, the corpses were unloaded at the

Okmulgee Furniture and Funeral Company. The posse immediately journeyed to the courthouse in order to file for the $3,000 in rewards offered for the bandit trio. An inquest, headed by a Police Judge O. K. Peck was held that afternoon. Peck ruled the trio's deaths a case of justifiable homicide. When interviewed by reporters on the courthouse steps, Sheriff Roach told how the ambush had played out. He claimed the outlaws had been armed with modern repeating rifles and pistols, and several hundred rounds of ammunition had been found in their tent. When asked where the bandits were coming from when they approached their camp on foot, he retorted that since the weather was so foul, he suspected the trio might have been sleeping in Pony Poe's barn nearby where they had taken refuge from the snowstorm. He guessed, when the sun came up, the trio must have decided to move back to their isolated camp at the spring, a half-mile distant. When the newsmen questioned Deputy Robbins about the events, he loudly stated in true old west fashion, the outlaws had "died game, with guns in their hands and lead in their bellies." Detective Gustavason informed the collection of in-

The old Okmulgee train depot, circa 1918. Site where Ms. Mabel Brooks Poe gave two of her many news conferences. Courtesy of the Okmulgee Public Library

quisitive correspondents, the ambush had been "a turkey shoot," he also commented, "while we were well concealed, the desperadoes were caught in the open" He further added it was "like shooting fish in a barrel."

The following day, newspapers as far away as Chicago, reported the Nuyaka gunfight in detail. Several papers incorrectly identified the location of the ambush as being deep in the confines of the Deep Fork Canyon, it seems they had gotten their information from a Tulsa reporter who had his spurs tangled. According to numerous sources, including one of the few remaining official documents relating to Sheriff Roach's tenure, other newspaper and magazine articles of the period, as well as decedents of citizens who lived in the area at the time of the ambush, the spring is the correct location of the ambush.

Several days after the Nuyaka ambush, Mabel Brooks Poe, Oscar's common-law widow came steaming into Okmulgee on the afternoon train. Reporters, tipped off to her arrival were waiting for her at the station. She was reportedly an attractive woman, dressed in fine attire. When questioned by the bevy of "newsies" about how she had gotten word of the ambush, she stated a reporter from the Coffeyville, Kansas newspaper had informed her of her husband's death. She went on to state, the reporter had asked if she would inform Jess Littrell's wife, who was the manager of a boarding house in town, of her husband's capture. She replied she wasn't acquainted with Mrs. Littrell and resented the implication that all bank robbers' wives should somehow know one another. When asked about Oscar's criminal career, she emphatically claimed she had tried to reform him many times, but he was a ship that could not be salvaged. She elaborated, Oscar's family was responsible for his life in crime, she further declared, and "they are a pack of thieves who are beyond redemption." When a newsman told her about the county's plan to plant her husband and his companions in pauper's graves, the widow replied she was going to make sure they were given decent burials, and further avowed she would also make sure Russell Tucker would be buried in the proper manner. The collection of reporters assured her, this detail was already taken care of by Tucker's next of kin. When quizzed about Jess Littrell's capture, she retorted it would have been better for him if he had been killed like the others; She elaborated, "A life in prison is no life at all." When asked what Oscar had done with all the stolen bank money she stomped off in a huff, making no comment on the subject.

The grieving widow, in all her finery (she was trailed by an entourage of three Black baggage handlers hired to tote her numerous trunks of fancy clothing), then made a beeline to the swankiest hotel in town. After freshening up and changing into an expensive silk dress and donning a hat capped with an ostrich feather, she made her way to

The unmarked grave sites of Oscar Poe and the two Hart brothers, Will and Harry, who were killed at the Nuyaka Ambush. Courtesy Naomi Morgan

the funeral home where her husband and the Hart boys were laid out. She reportedly gazed down at Oscar's face for about five minutes then turned to the undertaker, telling him she had brought clothing, suit and ties, which she wanted Oscar and Will Hart to be buried in. The widow also gave orders for the undertaker to buy suitable apparel for Harry Hart and arrange for three good coffins. She then pulled out a fat roll of bills, peeling off a couple of hundred dollar bills, telling the proprietor to see to the arrangements. When she inquired of the funeral director the exact details of the trio's deaths, she was directed to the good offices of Sheriff Claude Roach.

Followed by an army of reporters and curious onlookers Mabel made her way to the courthouse where Sheriff Roach invited her into his office. Roach explained in detail, the circumstances of the men's deaths. He also assured the widow the county had already purchased three grave plots in the town cemetery for the trio's internment. She asked the price of the plots. When told they cost a total of $21 she peeled off three tens stating she could not bear for the boys to be buried in common pauper's graves. With that, she dabbed an eye with a delicate pink lace hanky, sniffed, and bolted out the office door past the crowd of nosy correspondents, her head held high. An area reporter wrote, "You'd of thought she was the Queen of Sheba."

Back at the undertaking parlor, the three corpses were dressed and laid out in coffins, lined up side by side in the front parlor for public viewing. That evening and for the next two days over 1,500 citizens made their way through the parlor to gawk at the bandit's mortal remains. Lawmen escorted Centralia Banker T. R. Montgomery as well as Vinita Banker John Wise to officially identify the bodies of the trio as the robbers of their respective institutions. Both bankers took a quick look and positively identified Oscar Poe and Will Hart as two of the desperadoes who had ravaged their businesses. On Monday morning, Reverend J. B. Abernathy preached to the theme of "The wages of sin is death" to a crowd of about twenty people attending the trio's private funeral. The mourners included Oscar's aunt, Lizzie Poe, and her children, who lived only a half mile from the spot the trio were slain. Glaringly absent was Pony Poe, who was still enjoying the hospitality of the Nowata County jail. The Hart boys had no family in attendance, their mother, who lived in Centralia, had refused to claim their bodies or have anything to do with their funeral or burial. What motivated her to commit this seemingly heartless act is unknown. Decedents of the Harts claim it may have been the fact she did not want to be associated with her deceased children because of the social stigma attached to their being branded outlaws or perhaps it was because the widow was poor and ashamed she couldn't afford to contribute to their final expenses.

Later that afternoon, the three desperadoes were buried at the Okmulgee Park Cemetery side by side. Over 800 people attended the burial, which was open to the public. Shortly after the interment, Mrs. Poe made her way to the rail station where she prepared to board a northbound train. When reporters inquired if she would make a parting statement, she said, "It's sad it ended this way, but I knew Oscar would not be taken alive." When asked how she felt about facing charges of harboring and receiving stolen merchandise back in Kansas, she replied, "I once stopped the boys from shooting it out with the cops in Coffeyville." She elaborated, "No telling how many minions of the law they would have slain had it not been for my compassion. But for this act of charity on my part, I'm repaid by threats of jails and dungeons." She finished her statement by explaining, "A widow is not well treated in the state of Kansas." With that, she was gone.

Authorities in Kansas, where Mabel was under a $750 criminal bond, expressed the opinion that Mrs. Poe had paid for the bandit's burials with stolen money and would likely never arrive back in the "Sunflower" state to face the charges against her. It seems they were correct. Where she got off the train is unknown, but it wasn't in Kansas. How much of the gang's loot she possessed is also not clear. Mabel was not heard from again until early May when she showed up in Vinita, Oklahoma where she filed suit against Banker T. R. Montgomery demanding the Craig County court make him return the money she had turned over to the Coffeyville police in the fall of 1916. She claimed the money belonged not to the bank, (where it was obviously stolen from) but to her husband Oscar. She tearfully explained to the Judge, that as his still grieving widow the $1,190 was rightfully hers. The Judge, obviously not agreeing with her presumption, promptly dismissed her suit. Shortly after this court action, Mabel Brooks Poe disappeared into the mists of history never to be heard from again.

Chapter Seven

Sooner Justice

With the demise of Oscar Poe and the Harts, the gang as an organized unit was ended. The remnants of the group split to the four winds. The week following the Nuyaka ambush, Okfuskee Sheriff Barry Jones received information pointing to the whereabouts of two of the surviving gang members. It seems an elderly woman living near the small Okfuskee county settlement of Mason had been approached by two heavily armed men, whom she described as "seedy looking characters." They asked her for a meal, claiming they were cattle buyers from Kansas. The old lady later stated, "by their appearance they looked more like cattle rustlers than buyers," to her. She fed the men a ration of ham and eggs for which they paid her a dollar in change. Having recently gotten the word on the Boley and Nuyaka shoot outs, her suspicions were aroused by the presence of the strangers. When her neighbor, Sam Wilson, who was a part time constable, rode past her place the following day looking for a lost bull she informed him of her encounter with the men. Wilson, knowing officers were still seeking the whereabouts of the surviving members of the Poe-Hart Gang, decided to look into the matter. While searching the woods near the woman's home, he came across a cold camp where several persons had recently spent the night.

The following morning, a farmer rode into Mason complaining of the theft of two bay horses. That afternoon, a large mounted posse from Okemah led by Sheriff Jones and Constable Wilson, began scouring the timber near the farmer's residence located just east of the small village. On questioning other area ranchers, officers learned that numerous folks in the district had noticed a pair of saddle tramps hanging around the neighborhood the past few days. The descriptions gained from the witnesses matched those of gang members Lee Jarrett and Ab Connor. Jarrett's suspected presence in the area stirred up a great deal of interest since a $1000 cash reward was still in effect for his capture, dead or alive. Sheriff Jones suspected the pair had originally journeyed to the region attempting to link up with other gang members at their Nuyaka rendezvous site. Officers further speculated the pair had likely heard news of their fellow gang member's demise and were now on a scouting mission, searching for the missing loot from the robberies.

On the afternoon of January 28, a local rancher and his son sighted two men who matched the fugitive's description, mounted on what appeared to be bay horses, crossing a field north of Nuyaka. The Okemah posse, now joined by a large group of vigilantes from Okmulgee, raced

Old Mason store today. Courtesy of Naomi Morgan

Thippen J M—
Thomas J B—Okmulgee
Tiger S W—Mounds
Tiger Porter—Mounds
Vincent W A—Okmulgee
Webb N B—Okmulgee
Webb Gaither—Okmulgee
Webb Arthur—Okmulgee
Webb L W—Okmulgee
Webb W H—Inez N M
Webb Ernest—Okmulgee
Williams M C—Mounds
Webb T W—Okmulgee
Webb G W—Okmulgee
Williamson J W—
Williams M Z—Mounds
Waymire Frank—Mounds
Webber John—Mounds
Wilson W M—Mounds
Webb Myrtle May—Okmulgee
Webb L D—Okmulgee
Wilson W M—Okmulgee

PASCOE TOWNSHIP

Armstrong Geo—Beggs
Antwine Alsan—
Antwine Jule—
Abair W M—Beggs
Albro Ralph—Nuyaka
Andrews B D—Okmulgee
Alford Sigmond—Beggs
Alford G W—
Anderson O L—Nuyaka
Allen J A—Beggs
Allen W B—Beggs
Anderson O L—Nuyaka
Anderson Dickey—Beggs
Bacon Tom—Mounds
Bennett A B—Beggs
Benningfield E R—Beggs
Brown Marion—Beggs
Brown & Iron—Beggs
Bowman G W—Beggs
Brinkley H B—Beggs
Bell W C—Beggs
Banks Joe—Beggs
Blankenship G L—
Brown P I—Beggs
Bennett J B—Beggs
Barefoot M B—
Brown James—Beggs
Brooks E W—Beggs
Burney Joseph—Beggs
Barefoot B E—
Brunner Thos—Beggs
Burrow Thos—
Barber R F—Beggs
Clayton V D—Beggs
Clayton T M—Beggs
Clayton J R—Beggs
Copps J E—
Cankright W M—Beggs
Colbert M C—Beggs
Coleman James—Beggs
Crawford H C—
Coleman Peter—Beggs
Coleman Mary—Beggs

Carter W H—
Crossland Wm—Beggs
Clayton V D—Beggs
Clark Mollie Mrs—Nuyaka
Clark Clarence—Nuyaka
Cousins Nettie—Beggs
Cowan T J—Mounds
Cowan R B—Mounds
Cochran P A—
Dowland C H—Mounds
Davis Geo—
Dye D E—Nuyaka
Davis H C—Okmulgee
Dye E H—Nuyaka
Dancy Wade—Beggs
Dunn Albert—Beggs
Doyle Sam—Beggs
Dye J D—Nuyaka
Edmonson E E—Beggs
Eastham T W—Beggs
Everett Chas—Beggs
Fewell R P—Beggs
Friday Joe—Beggs
Fisher S M—Beggs
Foster E W—Beggs
Foster Mary J—Beggs
Foster E E—Beggs
Fewell C D—Beggs
Fewell J—Beggs
Galloway W M—Beggs
Grayson Thomas—Beggs
Grayson Geo—Beggs
Gaston Henry—Beggs
Galbraith A—Nuyaka
Griffin C H—Beggs
Gleason John—Beggs
Gleason W S—Beggs
Graham Rose—
Gibson J S—Beggs
Gunn B G—Beggs
Gains W L—Beggs
Harvey Albert—Beggs
Holmes C A—Mounds
Harvey J M—Beggs
Hubbell Fred—Beggs
Hubbell B H—Beggs
Hargrove C C—Beggs
Hance J B—Beggs
Hodge R J—
Hill S E—Beggs
Harris W L—Beggs
Hamilton G O—Mounds
Hotckiss C D—Mounds
Hamilton G C—Beggs
Hixon J F—Beggs
Hester Pete—
Hunter J H—
Herrod Miller—Beggs
Hanson L H—Beggs
Hanson John—Beggs
Johnson C R—Nuyaka
Johnson Pompey—Beggs
Johnson Soney—Beggs
James A B—Beggs
Jefferson M—Beggs
Jefferson Arthur—Beggs
Jones D H—Beggs
Komplen H J—Beggs

King Sam—Beggs
Lowery J H—Beggs
Lowery John—Beggs
Liggins Walter—Beggs
Lee R C—
Lunsford Martha—Beggs
Lachapelle Charlie—Beggs
Lunsford Ida—Beggs
Lunsford Paul—Beggs
Lunsford Hattie—Beggs
Lunsford Ben—Beggs
Luster C A—Beggs
Lankford T B Dr—Beggs
Lyons Henry—Beggs
Lunsford John—Beggs
Long J R—Beggs
Lyons Leonard—Beggs
Lewis Sherman—
Myer H D—Beggs
Myer W F—Beggs
Mercer J B—
Madewell Ben—Beggs
McClung F F—Beggs
McIntosh Robt—Beggs
Marbow L—
Major Frank—
McCann Lonnie—Nuyaka
McAfee Tom—
Martin W L—Beggs
Morris J L—Nuyaka
McIntosh Lizzie—Beggs
Mack Henry—Mounds
McEwen R B—Okmulgee
Madigan J F—
Martin Peter—Beggs
Nash Frank—Beggs
Orr M F—
Ockerman S H—Beggs
Ockerman L B—Beggs
Piper Jas—Beggs
Prince J W—Beggs
Phillips Arthur—Beggs
Pascol W J—Beggs
Phillips G A—Beggs
Poe A L—Nuyaka
Pendleton Al—Beggs
Pendleton Lawrence—Beggs
Pendleton Gus—Beggs
Pedigo W B—
Richards Sam—Beggs
Ross D L—Beggs
Rhodes John—Mounds
Rucker E M—
Roberts Henry—
Ralen Emery—
Rohl H W—Beggs
Rohl Pearl—Beggs
Rogers P R—Beggs
Sprinkle R W—Beggs
Sallee T W—Beggs
Salee R O—Beggs
St Cyr E—Beggs
Scott W—
Sexton J J—
Spriggs W E—Beggs
Stockton H S—Mounds
Sneed S D—
Soule P—Beggs

1918 Hoffhine's Okmulgee Directory, A. L. Poe listed in right column. Courtesy of the Okmulgee Library

to the area but after an intense search, which lasted several days, the posse gave up. Jones assumed the duo had given them the slip in the rugged canyon lands northwest of town.

Meanwhile, Buck George, one of the members of the posse who had eliminated Oscar Poe and the Harts, was given a hero's welcome back in Nowata. In the weeks following the Nuyaka ambush, the lawman's presence was in great demand as a speaker and guest of honor at get-togethers sponsored by numerous civic organizations in the area. He became a celebrity of sorts; telling and retelling his grisly tale while making the rounds on the local talk circuit. According to news reports, George had taken possession of Harry Hart's rifle, keeping it as a souvenir of the ambush. Reportedly, he was offered a great deal of money for the firearm, but refused to sell it. For reasons unknown, George loudly proclaimed Jess Littrell as the snitch who had informed lawmen of the gang's Nuyaka hideout. Littrell, who was currently a guest of the state in McAlester, in turn vigorously, denied the charge. As was discussed in the past chapter, there was at the time of the ambush a great controversy concerning the identity of the informant who directed lawmen to the exact site of the gang's final hideout. Okmulgee officers refused to name anyone as the songbird. Craig county authorities claimed Luther Cox; the young car thief who had escaped with Poe and Hart from the Vinita Jail was the Judas in the affair.

Although the name of the actual informant will probably never be known, there was a third man who could have easily been the dime dropper, Pony Poe. The forty-one-year old horse thief's dealings with the law throughout the case could be described as puzzling at best. For example, in December 1916, Poe was arrested in

Coffeyville at Oscar Poe's apartment after he attempted to flee from officers. He lied to police, denying he had accompanied the man and woman who had visited the residence the previous night. At the time of his apprehension, Poe was armed and carrying a great deal of cash money. Strangely, he volunteered to accompany officers to Vinita, Oklahoma to be questioned about any involvement he had with his nephew in the Centralia robbery. Within a few days, Poe was released from custody with no charges filed against him. Area newspapers quoted lawmen as saying he was granted his freedom due to his supplying the authorities with a great deal of helpful information. In December, Pony again involved himself in the case when he forked over $750 in cash to Montgomery County, Kansas officials to provide bond for Oscar Poe's wife, Mabel. Shortly after the pair left the state, authorities identified some of the bond money as originating from the recently robbed Alluwe, Oklahoma bank. Nowata County lawmen immediately traveled to Poe's Nuyaka ranch arresting him on a charge of possessing the stolen cash. Oddly, he was released from the Nowata county jail a few days after the Nuyaka shootout. As events unfold it appears obvious that Poe fit the "T" as a prime suspect for the role of informant in the case.

In February 1918, the Oklahoma Legislature voted to pay out the $500 a head reward for the killing and capture of Littrell, Tucker, Poe, and the Harts. Each of the seven Okmulgee posse men received about $200 apiece while the officers involved in the Boley ambush split a $1,000 amongst them. In March, the Oklahoma Banker's Association paid out $5,000 in reward money, which was split between both the Boley and Nuyaka posses. The widow of fatally wounded Deputy M. L. Boulware received a separate $1000 check.

In March of the same year, Nowata County Sheriff Bill Gillespey traveled to the Oklahoma State Prison with the intention of questioning the badly wounded Jess Littrell. On requesting to see the inmate, the prison warden at first refused, claiming the prisoner belonged to Okemah County. After a great deal of debate, the warden finally allowed him to visit the prisoner for thirty minutes. According to Gillespey, only a few words passed between the pair. The lawman asked Littrell if he would admit to his part in the slaying of the pair of officers in the Blue Canyon. The prisoner replied he would soon be proven innocent of those charges. Evidently, this response angered the Sheriff who retorted he would see Littrell hang one way or another. The outlaw, becoming sulky turned his face to the wall, ignoring the lawmen.

As 1917 dragged on, the wheels of justice slowly began tturning in the case. Joe Welsher, the individual who had given sanctuary to Tucker and Littrell in Harrah, was quickly tried and found guilty in Oklahoma County for harboring fugitives. He was sentenced to four years at the Oklahoma State pen. Bob Childers, who was accused of materially assisting the bandits while they were operating out of the Blue Canyon, also received a stiff prison sentence for his troubles.

Jess Littrell was finally well enough to go to trial in early October at Okemah for the murder of Deputy Boulware. A bond hearing was held where Littrell's attorney, a legal wiz named Carr from Paul's Valley, Oklahoma, who had been hired at great expense to Littrell's two brothers, who were both wealthy merchants from Hughes county, appealed to Judge John L. Norman for his client's release on bail. The Judge laughed at the attorney promptly denying his motion. A long and tedious trial began the following Monday. Numerous witnesses were called who implicated the defendant, but Littrell's slick attorney fought tooth and nail throughout the trial. Nothing was taken for granted. What looked like an open and shut case didn't evolve in that direction.

On presenting his case, Carr set forth a theory implying the bullet which killed Boulware had came from a fellow officers gun. In fact, he argued the point so vigorously the state was forced to exhume the corpse of the poor deputy and extract the projectile in an effort to prove it was the same caliber as those fired by Littrell. But alas, the round was so smashed or mushroomed the prosecutor could not disprove the charge. In the end, the jury could not reach a verdict and the Judge declared a hung jury. A retrial date of November 10 was set. Once again, Attorney Carr filed for bail. This time it was granted in the sum of $17,500. Littrell's brothers immediately put up $100,000 worth of property towards the bond. But the joke was on them. The Oklahoma County prosecutor quickly demanded Littrell be transferred to his jurisdiction to face a charge of robbing the Harrah Bank. The request was granted and the prisoner moved the next day to the county jail in Oklahoma City. Littrell's lawyer once more asked and received bail on the robbery charge, this time for the sum of $10,000. Again, the defendant's siblings came through putting up even more property to secure the bond. But, before the slippery outlaw made it out the jailhouse door, Nowata County authorities demanded his transfer to their county to face a double murder charge.

By this time, Littrell must have felt he couldn't win for losing. After setting but a few days in the Nowata County Jail, he was transferred back to Oklahoma County for trial on the armed robbery charge. The trial, which took less than a week, resulted in his being found guilty and sentenced to twenty-five years in the big house. The day after his conviction Littrell's bond was revoked and he was transferred to Okemah for his retrial for the murder of deputy Boulware.

On November 22, 1917, the befuddled bandit was convicted of first-degree murder and given a term of life in prison. Prison records indicate the outlaw was accepted at the Oklahoma State Penitentiary on November 26, as prisoner #8572, with a sentence of life and twenty-five years. Nowata County immediately put a hold on the prisoner so they would have the opportunity to try him for the deaths of Marshal Bullock and John Garretson, if he was ever released from prison.

On June 20, 1918, the missing Lee Jarrett, along with a seventeen-year-old thief named Will Creach and a Texas outlaw named Tom Slaughter, stole a Ford Touring car from Charles McGinnis near Centralia, Oklahoma. The following day they were arrested at the home of Jarrett's father, near Lenapah. Nowata County authorities were overjoyed with their catch. Jarrett was one of the most wanted men in Oklahoma at the time. He and his brother-inlaw were the last remaining active members of the Poe-Hart gang not dead or incarcerated. Slaughter, was wanted on a host of crimes in Texas.

The trio was arraigned in Nowata County district court on July 5 case #1458.

Tom Slaughter

Slaughter pled guilty to grand larceny but Jarrett and Creach claimed innocence. Amazingly, the Judge granted Jarrett his temporary freedom by an offer of $1,500 bond over the loud protests of C. F. Gowdy, the prosecuting attorney. Jarrett's brother Howard put up a car as collateral and Albert Connor's sister, Echo Connor, added 320 acres toward the bond. Slaughter and Creach were transported back to the county jail for safekeeping. Jarrett, who also had a warrant out for his arrest for bank robbery in nearby Craig County, immediately jumped bond heading to Joplin, Missouri, where he was arrested for auto theft the following week. Naturally, Jarrett, whose criminal minded family had connections at the courthouse in their hometown, quickly agreed to extradition to stand trial for the Oklahoma car theft charge. He was transported back to Nowata on July 10. The following evening, Jarrett and his fellow inmates, Slaughter and Creach, overpowered Jailors Lee Brady and James Hendrix. The trio quickly gained control of the jail's armory arming themselves with several rifles and a shotgun. They locked the lawmen in the cellblock before heading for freedom. After bolting out the front door of the basement jail, they made a beeline to a local garage where they stole a car, fleeing north out of town with a squall of rubber. Sheriff Gillespey quickly gathered two large posses and began pursuit of the fugitives. The following week, officers caught up with Creach in Centralia. Six weeks later, officers in Carter County Oklahoma nabbed Slaughter. He was promptly transported back to Nowata to face the music.

Since Slaughter was an extreme escape risk, Sheriff Gillespey decided to transfer him to a more secure facility in nearby Bartlesville. In the end the move proved fruitless, the slippery bandit sawed through the bars of his cell the following month making his way to freedom. Police soon lost track of the vicious outlaw, but his and Lee Jarrett's name continued to crop up on police blotters throughout the state due to their suspected involvement in several hi-jackings and armed robberies. Police in Nowata finally caught up with Lee Jarrett at the home of one of his nine brothers on February 8, 1920, but amazingly, his attorney again arranged bail in the form of another $1,500 put up by his brother, Howard, and Echo Connor. An outcry immediately went up from authorities in neighboring Craig County who wanted him held on charges of aiding Poe and Hart in their 1916 jail escape as well as his suspected complicity in the Vinita Bank robbery. By the time officers from that county arrived at the Jarrett farm there was no sign of the outlaw.

On October 15, 1920, Tom Slaughter and another man, suspected to have been either Lee Jarrett or Ab Connor, robbed the Bank of Alluwe in southern Nowata County. Slaughter was captured in Sedan, Kansas, ten days later. Instead of extraditing the criminal to Oklahoma where he faced a multitude of charges, he was transferred to Hot Springs, Arkansas, where he was wanted for the murder of a Deputy Sheriff. He again escaped jail on December 8,

Grave of Lee Jarrett. Photo by Naomi Morgan

1921, killing two men in the process. Later that day he was gunned down by officers near Benton, Arkansas. Lawmen breathed a sigh of relief on receiving news of the outlaw's death.

In May of 1921, the Nowata County court finally revoked the missing Lee Jarrett's $3,000 bond and issued a warrant for his arrest. In the proceeding months authorities suspected he, his brother Floyd and his brother-in-law, Albert Connor, along with a friend named Red Cloud Scruggs, a quarter blood Cherokee Indian, of knocking over a bank in Odessa, Missouri, as well as a couple of small general stores in Muskogee County, Oklahoma. Kansas authorities, which had dubbed the quartet, "The Cedar Creek Gang," also suspected the group's involvement in several robberies in their state.

On the evening of December 14, 1921 at around 11 p. m., Nowata County authorities received word of a nasty traffic accident occurring at the Cedar Creek Bridge, five miles east of Lenapah near the Jarrett Farm. When the ambulance and Sheriff's deputies arrived on the scene they were greeted by Bernard Jarrett and Albert's brother, John Connor who both lived nearby. Piled up on the bridge was a badly smashed Ford Touring car. Lying thirty yards away on the creek bank was the torn and mangled body of Lee Jarrett. On questioning the two witnesses, Connor and Jarrett stated they had come upon the accident while driving back from Lenapah, where they had been visiting friends. After sighting the smashed car, they investigated and found the victim in the middle of the creek. They pulled him out and Jarrett stayed with his brother while Connor drove to town and called an ambulance. Both claimed to know nothing else of the affair.

After a brief investigation, it came to light the story told by the two witnesses was bogus. It seems that the pair had lied to officers in an effort to protect the whereabouts of their kin, Albert Connor. As for the facts involving the deadly accident, it appears Albert and Lee Jarrett, both wanted for a host of crimes in the area, had been out "Tom Catting" around evidently drunker than skunks. After visiting some drinking buddies in nearby Lenapah, the pair was driving back to the Connor's farm when suddenly, Connor, who was at the wheel, lost control of the vehicle slamming into the bridge. Jarrett, riding in the car's passenger side was apparently ejected from his seat, his head striking the metal bridge railing. Authorities speculated the outlaw was killed on impact. The slightly injured Connor walked to the nearby Jarrett farm and informed Lee's brother Bernard and John Connor of the wreck, who in turn drove out to the scene where they found the victim and made up the tale they told police in order to protect Albert from capture.

Back in Okmulgee, John Lung was a happy man. After he and the other posse members were applauded by area newspapers, as well as the state legislature as heroes of the day and given what amounted to in those days a king's ransom in reward money their futures looked bright. In 1918, Melville Bowman resigned as Okmulgee Chief of Police creating an opening that seemed to have Lung's name written on it. He was immediately asked to fill the position, which he gladly accepted. In 1921, he resigned as chief and accepted a position as Chief Deputy under Okmulgee County Sheriff Frank Sowers. Later that year, he ran for a fourth time for the Sheriff's position. He was again defeated at the polls. Frustrated with public service, he opened up a private detective office in Okmulgee, although he still kept his hand in the Sheriff's department by requesting he be allowed to retain his deputy sheriff commission. Being in great need of his experience and steady hand with a pistol and billy club it was a request the new Sheriff gladly accepted.

Lung's first major case as a private dick involved the robbery of the Whitbeck-Dale Grocery in Okmulgee. The store's insurance company hired him in an attempt to regain possession of some $1,100 in cash and merchandise taken from the business in a midnight burglary, which had occurred the previous week. After a brief investigation, Lung had deducted the thieves were a group of nighttime yeggmen operating out of nearby Sapulpa in Creek County. The lawman also suspected the same band of thieves were responsible for a recent burglary in Tulsa, where the perpetrators had stolen nearly $10,000 worth of bonds from a business. This fact greatly interested Lung since there was a large reward offered for the return of the bonds. Within a matter of days, the detective tracked down one of the suspects at a Sapulpa residence. When Lung attempted to arrest the man the crook fired at him with a pistol, Lung returned fire shooting through a door the suspect was hiding behind. Although the rounds missed, it shook up the bad man enough to induce him to come out peaceably and

Grave of Albert Connor. Photo by Naomi Morgan

submit to arrest. The suspect, whose name turned out to be Hammond, was hauled to the Okmulgee jail where he made bond to the tune of $7,000 and was released.

On the evening of September 15, 1922, Lung, in the company of Sapulpa Chief of Police Ralph Morey spotted and began following a car they believed contained one of the suspects from the grocery store robbery. When the vehicle, a Ford sedan, containing a female driver and a single male passenger pulled into the Continental Garage in downtown Sapulpa the officers were hot on its tail. On observing the suspicious vehicle park in a dark corner of the garage, Chief Morey, who was driving, pulled up behind the rig blocking it's escape route. Lung approached the driver's side with pistol in hand while Morey covered the passenger side. Suddenly, a shot rang out from a shadowy corner of the garage. Morey turned toward his fellow officer thinking he had fired his pistol at one of the car's occupants. He stated he then observed Lung "pitch forward toward the concrete floor hitting face first." Morey heard two more shots coming from the same dark area the first shot had originated from. One of the bullets struck the ground directly in front of Moray's position; while the other passed by the officer's head so close, he heard it whistle. The Chief then claimed he heard a crash of glass and the shooting stopped. In the confusion, the man who was sitting in the suspect car fled the area, but Morey was able to capture his lady companion who was identified as sixteen-year-old Dora Stanley. Morey further stated, " We were lured into a classic ambush." Lung's assassin was later tentatively identified as a local hoodlum named Earl Pomeroy.

Within minutes of the shooting, witnesses called an ambulance, which quickly arrived on the scene. In his haste to get to a nearby hospital the driver of the meat wagon lost control of the rig crashing into a retaining wall a few blocks from the scene of the shooting. Another rescue vehicle had to be called. By the time of the arrival of the second ambulance, Lung had died. The medical examiner later stated the bullet that struck Lung had entered his right side breaking two ribs and passing through his lung before exiting his body. He also claimed the Deputy would not have survived even if he could have been transported to the hospital in a more timely manner.

On September 16, Lung's funeral was held at the Elks Lodge in Okmulgee. Several hundred citizens attended. He was buried at Okmulgee Park Cemetery later that afternoon only a short distance from where lie the mortal remains of Oscar Poe and the Hart boys. His wife and five children survived the forty-year-old lawman. The following week it was discovered Lung had taken out a $2,000 insurance policy on his himself. Sadly, the policy had not taken effect, since Lung had neglected to take the required physical. In the spring, the townspeople took up a collection and bought the rented home at 609 East 15th street where Lung's family had been living, making a gift of the residence to the widow in honor of her husband's service to the community.

Around this time, news of Ab Connor was received, when he, Earl and probably Floyd Jarrett robbed a store in Pryor, Oklahoma, stealing over $3,000 in cash and merchandise. On the morning of July 26, 1922, the same trio was suspected by lawmen to have robbed the bank at Lenapah. On March 24, 1923, Connor, in the company of Buster Jarrett and another thug named Max Webbe raided a small general store near Coffeyville, Kansas. Unluckily for them, the store owner, Robert Spriggs, was a battle hardened veteran of World War I. Shots were exchanged. When the gun smoke cleared, Connor and Webbe had both been struck repeatedly by bullets fired from the merchant's .38 caliber automatic pistol and were lying in the dirt street in intense agony. Jarrett dragged the pair to a waiting vehicle, driving the wounded men to a residence just south of town. After bedding down his wounded companions in crime, Buster split the scene. The following day, the debilitated pair of bandits got word through friends to the authorities, they were seeking to surrender in order to gain medical assistance. Both men succumbed to their wounds within days of their surrender. On April 4, 1923 Albert Connor was buried at the Ball Cemetery in Nowata County, Oklahoma. His wife, Hazel Jarrett Connor, and three children survived him. Incidentally, Connor's widow, Hazel, was later married for a short period to the notorious 1930s outlaw, Wilber Underhill. She died in California in 1979 and was cremated. Her ashes were buried next to her first love, Albert Connor.

THE STATE OF OKLAHOMA,

To the Sheriff of Nowata County:

Whereas, complaint in writing, and upon oath has been filed in the County Court of Nowata County, charging that *Lee Jarrett, Tom Slaughter and Will Creach* did on or about the ___*16th*___ day of ___*June*___ 191*8*, in the County of Nowata, State of Oklahoma, commit the crime of ___*Grand Larceny*___

You are therefore commanded forthwith to take said ___*Defendants*___ ___and bring him before me or some other magistrate having cognizance of the case to be dealt with according to law.

Given under my hand and the seal of the County Court of said County, this ___*5th*___ day of ___*July*___ 191*8*.

R.M. Godfrey
County Judge

Lee Jarrett, Tom Slaughter and Will Creach – auto theft, Nowata County, 1918.

RECORD OF FUNERAL.

No. _563_   No. _153_   Date _Sept. 16_ 1
(Total Number)   (Yearly Number)

Name of Deceased _John Lung_   _White_ (Where Born)
(What Race)

Wife—Widow or Son—Daughter or ....

Order Given by ....

Charge to. _E.P.O.E. 1136_

Price of Casket or Coffin _$70,000.00_ ...$ | _175_

How Secured ....

"   Metallic Lining ....

Address _Okemulgee_

"   Outside Box _____ (State kind) | _16_

Date of Funeral _Sept. 17 192_

"   Grave Vault _____ (State kind)

Residence _Okemulgee_

"   Burial Robe ....

Place of Death _Tulsa_

"   Burial Slippers and Hose........ | _2_

Funeral Services at _Elks Home_

Engraving Plate ....

Time of Funeral Service _2 P.M._

Embalming Body (with .... Fluid)

Clergyman _R.C. Vincent_

Washing and Dressing ....

Certifying Physician ....

Shaving ....

His Residence ....

Keeping Body on Ice...................

Number of Burial Certificate...........

Disinfecting Rooms ....

Cause of Death _Gun Shot Wound_
(Primary)   (Secondary)

Use of Catafalque and Drapery........

"   Folding Chairs ....

Date of Death _Sept. 15 192_

"   Candelabrum and Candles.....

Occupation of the Deceased _Oilman_

Gloves $........... Crape $.........

Single or Married.......... Religion ....

Door Crape $......... Canopy $........

Date of Birth.........................

Hearse........................... | _12_

Aged........ Years,........ Months,........ Days.

Carriages to Cemetery...... @ $........

Name of Father.........................

Automobiles to Cemetery.... @ $........

His Birthplace ....

Wagon Deliveries ....

Name of Mother........................
(Maiden Name)

City Calls (Coaches) ....

Her Birthplace ....

Death Notices in........ Newspapers........
(Names of Newspapers)

Body to be shipped to.................

Flowers ....

Size and Style of Casket or Coffin _grey gown_

Outlay for Lot.........................

6/3 x 425 S.S. half falcon

Opening Grave or Vault................

Manufactured by. _Ok. Casket Co._

Lining Grave ....

Interment at _Park_ Cemetery.

Evergreen ....

Lot or Grave No. _512_ Section No. _Q_

Tent or Awning Charges...............

Vault Rental ....

Shipping Charges, prepaid.............

Removal Charges ....

Cremation Charges ....

Porters $......... Watchers $.........

Personal Services .... | _1_

Music ....

Church Charges ....

Ambulance to Tulsa | _50_

Advance Ag S | _12_

Total Footing of Bill..........$ | _280_

By Amount Paid in Advance.............

Balance ..$.........

Entered into Ledger, page...........or below

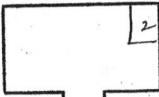

Diagram of Lot or Vault
Designate all Graves in Lot with Numbers (1, 2, 3, 4, etc.),
and mark space for this Funeral with a cross (+). _104_
Designate place for Monument with a small square ☐
Use space to the right of Diagram for the names of those buried in Lot.

1. ....
2. ....
3. ....
4. ....
5. ....
6. ....

Funeral record for John Lung

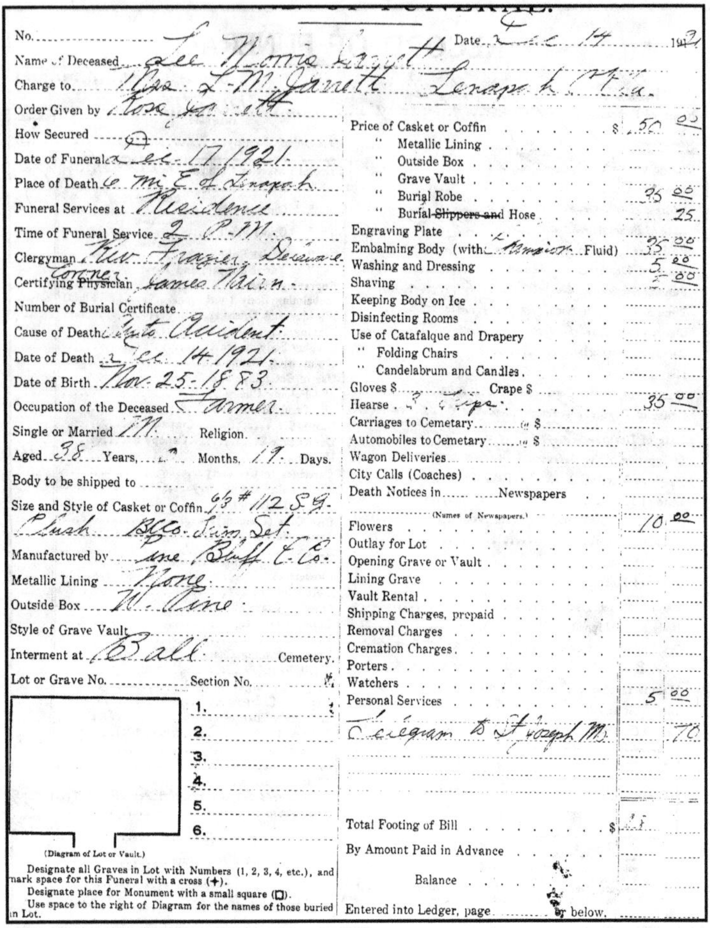

RECORD OF FUNERAL

No. .... Date Dec 14 1921

Name of Deceased Lee Morris Jarrett

Charge to Mrs L M Jarrett Lenapah Okla.

Order Given by Rose Jarrett

How Secured

Date of Funeral Dec 17 1921

Place of Death 6 mi E of Lenapah

Funeral Services at Residence

Time of Funeral Service 2 P.M.

Clergyman Rev. Frazier, Delaware

Certifying ~~Physician~~ Corner James Wain

Number of Burial Certificate

Cause of Death Auto Accident

Date of Death Dec 14 1921

Date of Birth Nov 25 1883

Occupation of the Deceased Farmer

Single or Married M. Religion.

Aged 38 Years, 0 Months, 19 Days.

Body to be shipped to

Size and Style of Casket or Coffin 6/3 #112 S.G. Plush Blk Co. Trim Set

Manufactured by Bluff C. Co.

Metallic Lining None

Outside Box W. Pine

Style of Grave Vault

Interment at Ball Cemetery.

Lot or Grave No. Section No.

1.
2.
3.
4.
5.
6.

(Diagram of Lot or Vault.)

Designate all Graves in Lot with Numbers (1, 2, 3, 4, etc.), and mark space for this Funeral with a cross (+).
Designate place for Monument with a small square (□).
Use space to the right of Diagram for the names of those buried in Lot.

Price of Casket or Coffin	$ 50 00
" Metallic Lining	
" Outside Box	
" Grave Vault	
" Burial Robe	35 00
" Burial ~~Slippers and~~ Hose	25
Engraving Plate	
Embalming Body (with Armour Fluid)	35 00
Washing and Dressing	5 00
Shaving	5 00
Keeping Body on Ice	
Disinfecting Rooms	
Use of Catafalque and Drapery	
" Folding Chairs	
" Candelabrum and Candles	
Gloves $ Crape $	
Hearse 3 trips	35 00
Carriages to Cemetary $	
Automobiles to Cemetary $	
Wagon Deliveries	
City Calls (Coaches)	
Death Notices in Newspapers (Names of Newspapers.)	
Flowers	10 00
Outlay for Lot	
Opening Grave or Vault	
Lining Grave	
Vault Rental	
Shipping Charges, prepaid	
Removal Charges	
Cremation Charges	
Porters	
Watchers	
Personal Services	5 00
Telegram to St Joseph Mo.	70
Total Footing of Bill	$
By Amount Paid in Advance	
Balance	
Entered into Ledger, page or below.	

Funeral record for Lee Jarrett.

RECORD OF FUNERAL.

No...._1_....
(Total Number)

No...._51_....
(Lot Number)

Date..._April 3._....19_23_

Name of Deceased............_Albert Conner_............ _White_ ....
(What Race) (Where Born)

Wife—Widow / Son—Daughter of }........_Mr. Mrs. James & Mrs. Conner_............	Order Given by........................			
Charge to	Price of Casket or Coffin..._Cut # 539_.....$	115	00
Address	" Metallic Lining		
How Secured	" Outside Box .... (State kind)		
Date of Funeral.......................	" Grave Vault .... (State kind)		
Residence	" Burial Robe	27	50
Place of Death.._Coffeyville Jail._....	" Burial Slippers and Hose............		
Funeral Services at._...._....	Engraving Plate		
Time of Funeral Service.._1.30_...	Embalming Body (with............Fluid)	25	00
Clergyman	Washing and Dressing............	5	00
Certifying Physician._D. Mills_....	Shaving		
His Residence	Keeping Body on Ice............		
Number of Burial Certificate............	Disinfecting Rooms		
Cause of Death._Peritonitis_....._5P._	Use of Catafalque and Drapery........		
(Primary) (Secondary)	" Folding Chairs		
Date of Death......._April 3 - 1923._	" Candelabrum and Candles........		
Occupation of the Deceased............	Gloves $...............Crape $........		
Single or Married..._M._....Religion	Door Crape $...........Canopy $........		
Date of Birth	Hearse............................	25	00
Aged..._5.8._Years,..........Months,........Days.	Carriages to Cemetery......@ $........		
Name of Father.......................	Automobiles to Cemetery....@ $.......		
His Birthplace	Wagon Deliveries		
Name of Mother....................... (Maiden Name)	City Calls (Coaches)............		
Her Birthplace	Death Notices in........Newspapers......		
Body to be shipped to........	(Names of Newspapers)		
Size and Style of Casket or Coffin...	Flowers	5	00
....	Outlay for Lot................		
Manufactured by_Rex Orla Christ Co._	Opening Grave or Vault........		
Interment at ....Cemetery.	Lining Grave		
Lot or Grave No............Section No........	Evergreen		
	Tent or Awning Charges........		
	Vault Rental		
	Shipping Charges, prepaid........		
	Removal Charges		
	Cremation Charges		
	Porters $...........Watchers $........		
1.	Personal Services ....._2.00_....	5	00
2.	Music		
3.	Church Charges		
4.	....		
5.	....		
6.	Total Footing of Bill........$	203	00
Diagram of Lot or Vault	By Amount Paid in Advance........		
Designate all Graves in Lot with Numbers (1, 2, 3, 4, etc.), and mark space for this Funeral with a cross (+). Designate place for Monument with a small square (☐) Use space to the right of Diagram for the names of those buried in Lot.	Balance		
	Entered into Ledger, page........or below		

Funeral record for Albert Conner.

Chapter Eight

Uncle Jim

As to the fate of Pony Poe, the suspected brains behind the Poe-Hart combination, he, unlike his companions managed to evade serious consequences for his actions. A few days after the bloody gunfight near his Nuyaka ranch, the forty-three-year-old miscreant was able obtain his freedom from the dreary confines of the Nowata County Jail when authorities there mysteriously dropped all pending charges and set him free. Whether he gained his liberty by way of legal maneuvering or a promise to testify against his fellow gang members is not known. The surviving legal documents on file in Nowata County are silent on the matter, although they do indicate he, his wife, and daughter were subpoenaed to testify in Jess Littrell's November 1917 double murder trial in that county. The subpoena requesting their testimonies was never consummated, due to Littrell's trial being put on hold. As was the custom in those days, Nowata County officials balked at wasting the taxpayer's money trying a man already convicted of the same crime elsewhere. Although Littrell had a life sentence plus twenty-five years hanging over his head, Nowata County did take the precaution of putting a hold on the outlaw, so they could try him in case he was ever released from prison.

What is known about the remainder of the elder Poe's turbulent life comes to us from official records and interviews conducted of several descendents of the bandit. It appears after the collapse of the gang as an organized unit he packed up his family and left Oklahoma, fleeing to

Wichita Falls, Texas, where in 1918 he changed his name and that of his family to Dotson (Dotson being his wife's maiden name). Whether this act of subterfuge was an attempt to hide from the law or his fellow surviving gang members is unclear. According to his descendents, soon after transplanting his wife and children to the "Lone Star" state, the outlaw began a lifetime habit of nomadic wandering. It appears he first drifted into New Mexico, where he joined his brother Cisero in the bootlegging business. There is also evidence suggesting he was employed as a truck driver in Oklahoma's Osage oil fields in the latter 1920s.

By all accounts, he was a poor provider, husband, and father. Luckily, for his wife, Lizzie, who remained in

Subpoena from Nowata County, Oklahoma, November 1917. Courtesy of the Nowata County Court Clerk's office.

Wichita Falls until her death, their children were mainly grown and able to attain work to support the family by this time. Poe's short visits back to the bosom of his family in Texas were few and far between. It's rumored he spent most of the depression working as a truck driver in Nebraska and Colorado.

Pony Poe or Jim Dotson, as he was known by then, is next heard from shortly before the advent of World War II. While serving a stretch at a prison farm in New Mexico on a theft charge, the old man was involved in a grisly murder of a fellow inmate. The story goes, Poe had gotten involved in a quarrel with an inmate who had loudly bragging to several other prisoners he was planning on killing the old bandit before his time was up. On the man's last day at the farm, he apparently attacked Poe with a ball pin hammer putting several permanent dents in his head before Poe turned and sliced his attacker from gut to gizzard with a knife he had been issued to cut baling twine. The wounded inmate died within minutes. Luckily for Poe, a guard had witnessed the event and testified the killing was an act of self-defense. After serving the remainder of his time, Poe traveled to California looking for work, which was plentiful during the war years.

In the last twenty years or more of his life, the old man was described as a shiftless, rolling stone of an individual. He spent his final years employed as a day laborer, a short order cook, and driving a truck in the oil patch.

Two of his descendents, a grandniece and nephew, tell of him visiting their homes numerous times over the years. Although both descendents came from different parts of the family, living many miles apart, they relay similar tales of his visits. According to them, "Uncle Jim," always drove an old truck with some type of camper shell on it, where he always slept, except on warm nights when he preferred sacking out on the ground in the open. He often showed up around harvest time and helped bring in the cotton. They remember a man who never cursed, drank, or gambled around them or their brothers and sisters and always having a pocketful of lemon drops which he freely passed out to the kids. During their childhoods, both relatives heard vague tales pertaining to "Uncle Jim" as once being some sort of an outlaw in the old days. According to a grandniece, she once spied a big horse pistol stuffed in a valise he always traveled with. She also tells of Poe promising her father to never come for a visit when he was wanted or on the scout from the law.

Photo of Pony Poe taken in Texas, circa 1940s. Courtesy of Nelda Poe Smith

As Pony grew older, he opened up to his grandnieces and nephews telling them of his adventures as an outlaw of the old west, although he never revealed his true name to them. Both agree, they always became excited when informed of his impending visits, admiring his tall tales and comparing him to the sagebrush heroes they saw every Saturday afternoon on the silver screen of the towns picture show. One of the stories he often told the children had to do with his knowing where "a pile of money was hidden," but alas he didn't dare go claim it, implying it would be too dangerous.

In his later years, after his wife Lizzie had died his sons reportedly made an effort to help the old man financially until they discovered he had been keeping a separate family in New Mexico secret from them for many years. On receipt of this information, his sons rarely welcomed him to their homes again or allowed him to have contact with his grandchildren. A granddaughter tells the story of when the old man did visit, his sons made him sleep in the home's attic. Whether it was because the boys feared he was wanted or just didn't care for his presence is unknown. Another tale told about Poe, implies that when he wore a black cowboy hat instead of a white one, everyone knew he was feeling cocky and was armed and ready. It appears he was a well-known character around Wichita Falls. Old timers remember him as a dangerous man whom most people made a great effort not to cross.

According to modern day Poe descendants, while Pony was visiting his daughter in the 1950s, the old man shot and killed her husband in a violent domestic quarrel. The shooting was declared a justifiable homicide at an inquest held several days after the event.

On February 16, 1963, the then eighty-seven-year-old Pony Poe was killed in a car accident in Ardmore, Oklahoma. At first authorities had grave difficulties identifying the aged man, it seems he had no drivers license but did possess three separate social security cards on his person. One of the cards identified him as James T. Dotson, another Jim Poe, and the third as Al Poe. The riddle was solved when a piece of paper was found with the name

FUNERALS

Jim (Pony) Poe
Arrangements are incomplete at Bettes Funeral Home for Jim (Pony) Poe, who died Monday morning in a local hospital.

Pony Poe's obituary in the February 22, 1963, Daily Ardmorite. Courtesy of Bettes Funeral Home Ardmore, Oklahoma

and telephone number of one of his nephews. When contacted by authorities, the nephew, who was one of the few people Pony had confided in about his past, informed officers the deceased name was "Pony" Poe. He also gave police the names of Pony's children. When they were contacted, they expressed no interest in the dearly departed. On February 21, 1963, Poe was buried in an unmarked pauper's grave at Ardmore's Rose Hill cemetery. The funeral home employees acted as mourners and pallbearers.

Years later, when the last of Pony's sons died and his grandchildren (who had grown up under the name of Dotson) were going through an old battered chest, which belonged to Pony's wife, Lizzie, and had been stored in the attic for many years, they made a shocking discovery. Inside the dusty box, family members found wrapped in a piece of twine, a pile of old news clippings, yellowed with age and brittle to the touch which told the story of the Poe-Hart Gang and their Oklahoma crime spree of over a half century past. These articles and other discovered documents gave the names of those involved as Poes not Dotsons. When younger family members, who had been kept in the dark for decades showed these documents to an elderly Aunt, she explained the ugly facts behind an earlier generation of bank robbers, horse thieves, and murderers.

Funeral record for Pone Poe.

Epilogue

As to the fates of the other major players involved in this short but tragic chapter in Oklahoma history, Okmulgee County Sheriff Claude Roach took ill shortly after the Poe-Hart ambush and moved in with his children in Portland, Oregon. He died there in April 1920. He is buried at the Okmulgee Park Cemetery.

Deputy Sheriff W. R. Robbins left the Sheriff's department in 1920, securing a job as a tax collector. In 1928, he bought a farm in rural Okmulgee County, farming and raising stock for the next twenty-two years. He died of a heart attack on January 24, 1950. He was buried at Okmulgee Park Cemetery. Robbins was one of the last survivors of that legendary breed of western lawmen made famous in song and film.

Grave of Sheriff Claud Roach. Photo by Naomi Morgan

Lee Jarrett's younger brother, Earl, was briefly named to the FBIs 10 most wanted list after his escape from the Oklahoma State Prison where he was being held for the murder of a federal officer, as ,well as several bank robberies.

In October 1929, Jess Littrell, having served his time (due to his accumulated good time and a lax parole board) for the murder of Deputy Boulware and the Harrah bank robbery, was transported to Nowata, Oklahoma to be tried for the murder of John Garritson and Charles Bullock. When Charles Barham, the state's chief witness, was unable to positively identify Littrell as one of the shooters, Judge Hal Johnson instructed the jury to return a verdict of not guilty stemming from insufficient evidence. According to an area newspaper, the District Attorney made only a halfhearted effort through out the proceedings and several key witnesses for the prosecution were glaringly absent from the trail. He was granted a provisional parole from the Oklahoma State Penitentiary two years later on July 17, 1931. Although authorities suspected his involvement with depression era gangsters "Big" Bob Brady, Ed Davis, Bill Shipley, and Jim Clark in the June 16, 1933 armed robbery of the State Bank in Black Oak, Arkansas,

Grave of Officer Robbins. Photo by Naomi Morgan

he was awarded a full pardon on November 5, 1934. It appears he never returned to prison and rumor has it he died in the 1960s.

Although the destructive hands of man and the degrading forces of nature have changed the face of the land over the past eight and a half decades, the physical trail of the Poe-Hart Gang and the Lawmen who defeated them can still be followed, if one looks hard enough. For those who are interested, the next few pages contain a short travelogue of the major sites referred to throughout the book.

The Blue Canyon country, which encompasses a large slice of Craig and Nowata County, Oklahoma, is still a place of vast rolling prairies dotted with scenic eruptions of picturesque bald buttes. It is now, as it was eighty years ago, an isolated, sparsely populated district mainly occupied by huge cattle ranches. Located nearby is the modern day ghost town of Centralia. Once a thriving business center, now inhabited by only a few dozen souls, the town's demise was directly tied to being bypassed by the railroad and the areas small farms being taken over by the major ranching concerns. Although the building which housed the bank that the gang robbed has long been torn down, the old

FATHER
ETHAN A.
SPENCER
DEC. 26. 1887
SEPT. 20. 1923

Final resting place of outlaw Al Spencer, Nowata County, Oklahoma. Courtesy of Naomi Morgan

square and it's turn of the century row of crumbling brick buildings offer a visual treat to any tourist interested in old west history and architecture.

In the nearby town of Vinita, the Farmers State Bank building has survived, but is now a law office. The jail where Oscar Poe and Will Hart escaped still stands. Although it has been converted into a private office building, the dark, damp dungeons located in an unused section of the buildings basement essentially appear today as they did eighty-odd years ago.

Thirty miles west, in the city of Nowata, the stately courthouse and jail where several of the gang members were lodged and stood trial, stands as a testament to the good taste of our ancestors when constructing public buildings. South of town lies the mortal remains of Russell Tucker, while several miles northeast of the city the graves of Walter and Lee Jarrett, along with Ab Connor can be found at the Ball Cemetery. Incidentally, the cemetery also holds the remains of infamous 1920s bandits Al Spencer and Dick Gregg.

Remains of old stone barn where shootout occurred near IXL.
Courtesy of Naomi Morgan

Due north of Nowata lies the historic city of Coffeyville, Kansas. The Isham Hardware Store, which is still in business, stands in the city's old public square next to the well-preserved Condon Bank where the Dalton Boys met their Waterloo in 1892.

Fifteen miles northwest of Okmulgee, Oklahoma, which is located in the east-central part of the state, there lies the unmarked graves of Oscar Poe and the Harts as well as John Lung, the hard bitten lawmen who proved to be their nemesis in battle. Fifteen miles west of town, near the banks of the Deep Fork Canadian River, sits the historic nineteenth century Nuyaka Mission. A half mile walk across a cattle pasture; one can still see the wooded spring where Oscar Poe and the Harts met their ends. Just to the west of the mission is the location of Pony Poe's farm, only an abandoned well marks the spot.

Twenty miles southwest of Nuyaka is the location of the now defunct community of IXL (I excel). All that remains of the old schoolhouse is the ruins of a retaining wall and a nearby root cellar. A mile and a half west of the present fire station one sees the foundations of a large rock barn located just off the road, which marks the site of the

Modern Day view of site of the IXL schoolhouse.
Courtesy of R. D. Morgan

shootout where Deputy Boulware and Russell Tucker lost their lives. A long time resident told the author of how as a child he and his friends would use their pocketknives to cut the spent lead bullets out of the nearby blackjack trees for use as fishing sinkers.

Family Reunion

One of the most unusual "family reunions" in history took place Saturday May 17, 2003 in Bartlesville when relatives of an early-day Oklahoma outlaw gang gathered at a local bookstore.

At least four distant relatives of the unsavory subjects of a written history of "the Poe-Hart gang" agreed to attend a book-signing event at Hastings Books, Music & Video.

While it was the first time the relatives met, it was considered to be a "reunion" of sorts.

Those planning to attend include Joe R. Tucker of Bartlesville, 75, a retired branch manager for Phillips Petroleum Company; and Archie Collins of Davis, also 75 and a retired Army sergeant.

Tucker is a nephew of outlaw gang member Russell Tucker, who was killed in a shoot-out with lawmen in Okfuskee County 1917.

"He was killed about 11 years before I was born, and my dad would never say much about him," Tucker said – adding, however, that he's excited about the upcoming meeting with the others. "It's history – it's something that happened," he said.

Collins said his second cousins Harry and Will Hart, who were bank robbers known as "the Hart twins," were both killed in gun battles with lawmen in Okmulgee County in 1917 – "and they both were buried there with their boots on, so to speak."

Reunion modern day decendants of Poe-Hart Gang.
Front: Nelda Poe Smith Back: Archie Collins, Author R. D. Morgan
and Joe Tucker. Courtesy Naomi Morgan.

Also attending the bookstore event was Bobby Dale Poe, 76-year-old farmer of Lometa, Texas, and Nelda Poe Smith, a retired teacher of Lampasas, Texas, great-nephew and great great niece respectively of Adolphus Lane "Pony" Poe.

Betty Poe attended the book signing with husband Bobby Dale Poe, expressed excitement about the event.

"I'm kind of anxious to meet some of the other relatives of these outlaw gangs," she said, adding that she personally recalls the outlaw Pony Poe, whom she knew better as "Uncle Jim."

"I can remember Uncle Jim visiting us when our children were small," she said, "and I watched the kids pretty close when he visited because it was known that he carried weapons and didn't want children prowling in his pickup because of it."

Betty Poe explained that outlaw Adolphus Poe, who also had the nickname of "Pone" and for years used the alias of James T. "Jim" Dotson (using the maiden name of his wife, Mary Elizabeth), was born in Travis County, Texas, in 1876.

She said that after he spent time in prison and "on the owl-hoot trail," he died as result of an auto accident in Ardmore in 1963 at the age of 86.

Author Morgan, of Haskell, a 48-year-old former government employee, who invited the outlaws' relatives to the book signing, called them "respectable citizen types … and dedicated genealogists."

"Most folks in Oklahoma and Texas don't mind having outlaws in their family tree as long as a few decades have past," he said.

Reunion: Front: Nelda Poe Smith and Betty Poe.
Back: Author R. D. Morgan, Joe Tucker and Bobby Dale Poe.
Courtesy Naomi Morgan.

Bibliography

Books:
Okmulgee County History, Okmulgee Historical Society, Historical Enterprises Inc., Tulsa, Oklahoma
DeMoss, Robert, "A Look at the History of Nowata Oklahoma," Nowata Historical Museum
Owens, Ron, "Oklahoma Justice, The Oklahoma City Police," Turner Publishing Co., Paducah, Kentucky.

Articles and Periodicals:
Hoffhines Okmulgee City Directories, 1909-1923
Butler, Ken, "Outlaw Tom Slaughter, Even His Name Spelled Death" Oklahombres Journal, 1998
Kirkland, Barbara and Gerald, "Boulware Family History"
Mattix, Rick, "Big Bob Brady: Forgotten Depression Outlaw", Oklahombres Journal, 1997

Newspapers:
Vinita Leader
Haskell News
Tulsa Daily World
Muskogee Phoenix
Muskogee Times-Democrat
Coffeyville Daily Journal
The Delaware Register
Joplin Globe
Lenapah Post

Claremore Daily Progress
Henryetta Daily Free Lance
Morris News
The Daily Oklahoman
Nowata Weekly Star
Okmulgee Chieftain
Okemah Ledger
Okfuskee County News
Sapulpa Herald
Tulsa Democrat
Henryetta Standard

Appreciation is expressed to the following organizations for the use of their historical records, documents, microfilm, and archives:

Craig County Court Clerks office Vinita, Oklahoma
Okmulgee County Court Clerk Okmulgee, Oklahoma
Office of the Court Clerk Nowata County, Nowata, Oklahoma
Oklahoma Department of Corrections
Kansas Department of Corrections
Craig County Sheriff's Department-Jim Herman
Shurden-Kelley Funeral Home, Okmulgee, Oklahoma, Tina Clonts
Okmulgee Park Cemetery Offices Okmulgee, Oklahoma
Benjamin Funeral Home Nowata, Oklahoma
Coffeyville Public Library Coffeyville, Kansas
Muskogee Public Library Muskogee, Oklahoma
Okemah Public Library Okemah, Oklahoma
Tulsa Public Library Tulsa, Oklahoma
Vinita Public Library Vinita, Oklahoma
Nowata Public Library Nowata, Oklahoma

Joplin Public Library, Joplin, Missouri
Okmulgee Public Library Okmulgee, Oklahoma
Phoenix Coal Sales Inc. Vinita, Oklahoma
The Nuyaka Mission Alumni Association Nuyaka, Oklahoma
The Eastern Trails Museum Vinita, Oklahoma
Creek Council House Okmulgee, Oklahoma
Okfuskee County Historical Museum, Okemah, Oklahoma

Special Titles from New Forums Press

call 1-800-606-3766 or go to www.newforums.com to order!

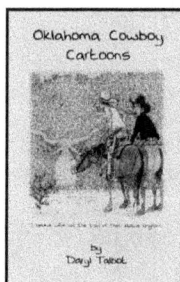

Oklahoma Cowboy Cartoons
–by Daryl Talbot

Award-winning cartoonist Daryl Talbot returns with this collection of cartoons depicting the funny side of modern cowboyin'. If you've ever owned a horse or worked on a ranch (or wished you did), you'll get a kick out of this lighthearted look at ranchin' and ropin'.
1999 (ISBN: 1-58107-014-4; 64 pages, 5 1/2 x 8 1/2, soft cover) **$ 7.95**

Between Me & You & the Gatepost— Rural Expressions of Oklahoma
(2nd, enlarged edition)
–by Jim Etter, illustrated by Daryl Talbot

A new and bigger edition of this popular collection of homegrown expressions and euphemisms that have distinguished the speech of Oklahoma folks for a coon's age and may do so 'til the cows come home. Take the bull by the horns and buy this book, and you'll be grinnin' like a possum eatin' persimmons!
1999 (ISBN: 1-58107-015-2; 44 pages, 5 1/2 x 8 1/2, soft cover) **$ 7.95**

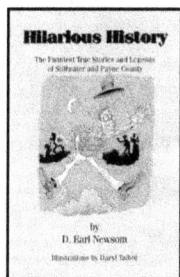

Hilarious History: The Funniest True Stories and Legends of Stillwater and Payne County
-by D. Earl Newsom

A collection of many true stories of the early days of Stillwater and Payne County that in retrospect are hilarious, although they often involved bitter controversies at the time: adultery, fist-fighting attorneys, bootlegging preachers, and preachers' bitter debates (and fist fights). Taken from contemporary newspaper accounts.
1999 (ISBN: 1-58107-016-0; 60 pages, 5 1/2 x 8 1/2, soft cover) **$ 7.95**

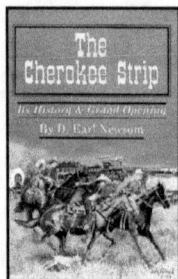

The Cherokee Strip—Its History & Grand Opening

–by D. Earl Newsom

The opening of the Cherokee Outlet, popularly known as the Cherokee Strip, on September 16, 1893, was one of the great spectacles of American history. Relive the excitement in this outstanding volume. Includes a history of the Cherokee Nation; the towns of Alma, Blackwell, Enid, Newkirk, Perry, Ponca City, and Woodward, along with the 101 Ranch. Illustrated with 160 historical photographs.

1992 (ISBN: 0-913507-27-X; 209 pages, 6 x 9 inch, soft cover) $13.95

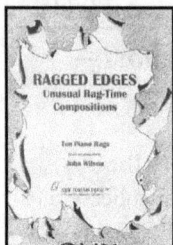

Ragged Edges: Unusual Rag-Time Compositions

–by John Wilson

Here is a true delight for those interested in early Oklahoma history. Ragtime was the music of the period of the land-run and early statehood , the music that inspired, entertained, and delighted the pioneer forefathers of Oklahoma! You will be tapping your feet to Professor Wilson's skillful rendering of Eli Green's Cake Walk, Mandy's Ragtime Waltz, The Watermelon Trust Slow Drag, and others. And, those who play the piano will certainly enjoy trying their fingers at these invigorating tunes. **Includes audio cassette.**

1998 (ISBN: 0-913507-98-0; 122 pages, 8 1/2 x 11, soft cover, lay-flat binding) $25.00

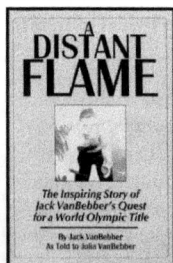

A Distant Flame: The Inspiring Story of Jack VanBebber's Quest for a World Olympic Title

–by Jack VanBebber as told to Julia VanBebber

The autobiography of a sickly and partially handicapped Oklahoma boy who developed his abilities to become an NCAA champion wrestler at Oklahoma A&M, win a 1932 Olympic Gold Medal, and eventually be known as one of the ten greatest amateur wrestlers of all times. A must for young readers and sports fans.

1992 (ISBN: 0-913507-26-1; 192 pages , 5 1/2 x 8 1/2, soft cover) $13.95

The Story of Exciting Payne County
– by D. Earl Newsom

A virtual encyclopedia of Payne County, its towns and villages, and its people since the 1889 land run. Included are detailed histories of the major towns (Stillwater, Cushing, Perkins, Yale, Glencoe, and Ripley), histories of the once thriving oil towns, brief histories of more than 20 villages that have virtually disappeared, maps, photos, lists of county officials, and dates of major events in every community.
1997 (ISBN: 0-913507-91-1; 272 pages, 8 1/2 x 11 inch, hard cover)   *$29.95*

Stillwater History - The Missing Links
-by D. Earl Newsom

Fascinating events, Stories and Pictures not included in Previous Books. D. Earl Newsom's final book dealing with Stillwater history and at his request a limited edition was published. The Madeline Webb Murder Trial, the Mathews Murder Case, the Ku Klux Klan, Stillwater's Movie Histories, "Doc" Whittenberg, the Ramsey Oilfield,Stories behind Street Names and Hotels, Taxis and Buses.
2000 (ISBN: 1-58107-027-6; 72 pages, 8 1/2 x 11 inch, soft cover)   *$15.95*

Claiming the Unassigned Lands
-by Clyde Shroyer

Mr. Shroyer has researched and gathered family information, backing it up with historical research to accomplish the task of telling his family story and their role in Oklahoma History. Recommended by the 1889er Society
2000 (ISBN: 1-58107-025-X, 390 pages, 5 1/2 x 8 1/2, soft cover)   *$19.95*

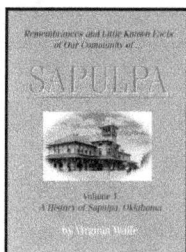

Remembrances of Sapulpa (Vol 1.)
-by Virginia Wolfe

Compiled from the author's weekly column for the *Sapulpa Daily Herald* celebrating Sapulpa's centennial, this first volume of a projected ten-volume series tells the story of Sapulpa's growth and development as seen through the eyes of many of its founding families and leading citizens. Liberally illustrated. A real nostalgia trip!

1998 (ISBN: 1-58107-010-1; 138 pages, 8 1/2 x 11 inch, soft cover)   **$25.00**

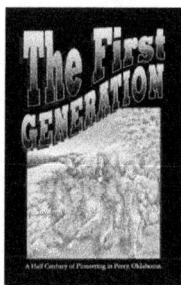

The First Generation—A Half Century of Pioneering in Perry, Oklahoma
-by Fred G. Beers

A glimpse at the earliest days of Perry, Oklahoma, and the Charles Machine Works, Inc., the manufacturer of Ditch Witch® equipment, through five decades from a bald, treeless prairie at the middle of the great land rush of 1893 to today's bustling, verdant community populated by picturesque descendants of hardy pioneer stock.

1991 (ISBN: 0-913507-22-9; 384 pages, 6 x 9, hard cover)   **$19.95**

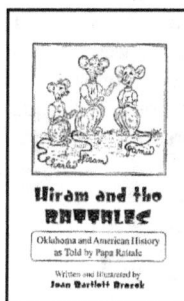

Hiram and the Rattales
-written and illustrated by Joan Bartlett Brozek

A unique look at Oklahoma and American history as seen through the eyes of a special family of rats living in southern Oklahoma. Papa Rattale tells his children the stories of the great events of American history as handed down to him by his ancestors. A book that makes American and Oklahoma history come alive for the young and the young at heart.

1988 (ISBN: 1-913507-39-3; 90 pages, 5 1/2 x 8 1/2, soft cover)   **$ 7.95**

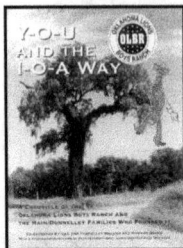

Y-O-U and The I-O-A Way
-by Lea Ann Donnelley Walker
and Richard Green

A chronicle of the Oklahoma Lions Boy's Ranch, its philosophy, and the Main and Donnelley families who founded it, told by the daughter of cofounder H.F. Donnelley. Liberally illustrated, including many facsimile documents. Proceeds from the sale go to support of future programs of the Ranch.

1998 (ISBN: 0-913507-90-3; 170 pages, 8 1/2 x 11, soft cover)   *$20.00*

Thunder in the Heartland –
Parables from Oklahoma
-by Jim Marion Etter

Just as truth is often stranger than fiction, sometimes it takes a touch of fable to give a true story the luster of immortality. At least, this seems so with Oklahoma, where, except for monumental events like the 1995 Oklahoma City bombing, many significant moments in history have been largely forgotten. They have been left to sleep in the memories of a few and on microfilmed pages of yesteryear's newspapers, in obscure library books or in dusty court records.

Except for the one based on the bombing itself, the following stories, all of which are fiction inspired by fact, are an attempt to awaken a few of these happenings, circumstances and traditions that in fact *are* the Sooner State. Any similarity between some fictitious name and that of a real person, of course, is a flat accident.

Author Jim Etter has completed an excellent collection of compelling stories with which all Oklahomans can identify. A must for your reading pleasure!

2000 (ISBN: 0-58107-034-9; 214 pages, 5 1/2 x 8 1/2, soft cover)   *$14.95*

Here's the perfect guide to take you down memory lane as you drive the most famous nostalgic route in history –

Route 66

in Oklahoma!

Featuring
- An in-depth essay on music from Oklahoma
- Notable music histories of Oklahoma cities, towns, and tribes on Route 66
- Notable musicians from Oklahoma Cities and towns on Route 66
- Where to hear live music, sing karaoke, and find a good jukebox
- Annual music events along Route 66 in Oklahoma
- Museums and other places with a musical focus
- Route 66 Maps for the U.S., Oklahoma, and tribal nations in Oklahoma
- Where to collect vinyl and other music memorabilia

2004 (ISBN: 1-58107-090; 200 pages, 5 1/4 x 8 1/4) $10.95

The Bandit Kings of the Cookson Hills

Author R. D. Morgan chronicles the true adventures of a loose-knit confederation of daring bank bandits originating from the infamous Cookson Hills of Eastern Oklahoma who terrorized the Arkansas-Oklahoma borderlands for more than a half decade following the close of the First World War.

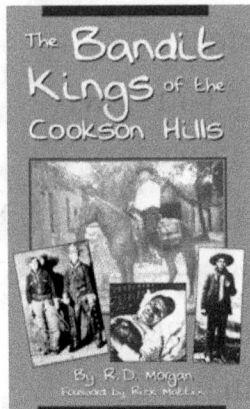

The original leader of the group was Henry Starr, the Cherokee bandit, who claimed to have robbed more banks than any man. Upon his death, a middle-age storekeeper along with an audacious young war hero named Ed Lockhart took over the helm.

In a time when most Americans were captivated by the "Teapot Dome" scandal, the death of President Harding, and the gridiron adventures of Notre Dame's "Four Horsemen," folks living in the Ozark Mountains watched with fear and fascination as the outlaw band committed their bold depravations. Although the gang's take rarely amounted to over $2000, it must be remembered the average yearly income for a family of five in 1922 amounted to $2100. A gallon of gas cost eleven-cents and a loaf of bread fetched only nine pennies.

2003 [ISBN: 1-58107-082-9; 5 1/4 x 8 1/4 inch]   **13.95**

The Bad Boys of the Cookson Hills

Their reign of terror lasted 18 long months!

R. D. Morgan continues the stranger-than-fiction true tale of the Cookson Hills Bandits. Here is a detailed description of a vicious crime and the eighteen-month long manhunt to track down the criminals involved. It details the history and crimes of a loose-knit gang of bold outlaws originally known as the Cookson Hills Gang, then the Ford Bradshaw Gang and finally the Underhill-Bradshaw Gang whose members blazed a path of robbery and murder through Oklahoma, Kansas, Nebraska, and Arkansas in 1932-34. It also chronicles the efforts and sacrifices of a handful of brave lawmen that tracked them down.

2002 [ISBN: 1-58107-059-4; 5 1/4 by 8 1/4 inch]   **$13.95**